A Frank Boreham Treasury

A
Frank Boreham
Treasury

compiled by

Peter F. Gunther

MOODY PRESS

CHICAGO

With permission of Epworth Press, London, selected chapters from the
works of Frank W. Boreham have been excerpted as follows:

From *A Bunch of Everlastings* (©1920, 1929): "Martin Luther," "Hugh
Latimer," "John Knox," "Oliver Cromwell," "John Bunyan," "John
Wesley," "John Newton," "William Carey," "Thomas Chalmers," "David
Livingstone," and "Charles Spurgeon."

From *A Handful of Stars* (©1922): "Catherine Booth," "James Hudson
Taylor," and "James Chalmers."

From *A Casket of Cameos* (©1924): "George Whitefield" and "John G.
Paton."

From *A Temple of Topaz* (©1928, 1933): "William Tyndale" and
"Adoniram Judson."

From *A Faggot of Torches* (©1926, 1933): "Blaise Pascal."

Library of Congress Cataloging in Publication Data

Boreham, Frank, 1871-1959.
    A Frank Boreham treasury.

    1. Christian biography.   2. Clergy—Biography.
I. Gunther, Peter F.   II. Title.
BR1700.2.B63   1984   270'.092'2 [B]   84-4594
ISBN 0-8024-0364-6

1 2 3 4 5 6 7 Printing/BC/Year 89 88 87 86 85 84

Printed in the United States of America

Contents

Foreword

On Sunday evening, May 21, 1911, the pastor of the Baptist Tabernacle in Hobart, Tasmania, announced a series of sermons that was as much a surprise to him as to the congregation. He had already announced a biweekly series on "The Specters of the Mind" and wanted to encourage the people to attend on the alternate Sundays as well. He found himself announcing a series on "Texts That Made History," with "Martin Luther's Text" as the very first message. (The previous week he had read a new biography of Luther, so the great Reformer was on his mind.) Before the series ended, he preached one hundred and twenty-five sermons. It turned out to be his most popular sermon series.

The preacher was Dr. Frank W. Boreham, and the series was published in five volumes from 1920 to 1928: *A Bunch of Everlastings, A Handful of Stars, A Casket of Cameos, A Faggot of Torches,* and *A Temple of Topaz.* It is perhaps one of the most famous series of sermons in the history of preaching and certainly one of the most original.

Frank W. Boreham was born on March 3, 1871, in Tunbridge Wells, England. He became an avid reader at an early age and was encouraged by his father to read the best biographies, a practice Boreham continued all his life. His schooling finished, he worked at various business offices in London, was converted and united with a local Baptist church, began to preach, and then felt a definite call to the ministry.

He was probably the last student that Charles Haddon Spurgeon personally interviewed for entrance into his Pastors' College.

After graduation Boreham accepted a call to a church in New Zealand. He began his ministry at the Mosgiel Baptist Church, Dunedin, in March 1895, and quickly won the hearts of the people. He also began to write essays for newspapers as an extension of his ministry and soon became a popular "local writer." Many of these delightful essays were eventually included in the more than forty books that Boreham was to publish during his lifetime, books that I heartily recommend to you. I agree with Dr. John Henry Jowett, who said, "I would advise you to read all the books of F. W. Boreham!"

Boreham pastored Baptist churches in Hobart, Tasmania, and Melbourne, Australia; and then left the pastoral ministry to devote himself to itinerant preaching and writing. He traveled widely and preached to large and appreciative congregations. He was once introduced as "the man whose name is on all our lips, whose books are on all our shelves, and whose illustrations are in all our sermons." One pastor confessed that he would be ashamed to meet Boreham personally, having "borrowed" so much of his material for his own sermons.

One of his closest friends wrote of Boreham, "Nobody saw him in a hurry, and nobody saw him idle." He was punctually at his desk each morning at 8:30 and at lunch each afternoon at 1:00. For one hour after lunch he went to bed and slept soundly; then he set out for his afternoon of visitation. He set aside each Thursday afternoon and evening for "an outing" with his wife, and in the midst of pastoral duties he managed to read at least one book a week and publish at least a book a year.

His forty-sixth book, *The Tide Comes In*, was published in 1958. On May 18, 1959, F. W. Boreham was called Home. He was buried at the Kew Cemetery in Melbourne.

Some of Boreham's books have been reprinted from time to time, but many of them have become collectors' items. I rejoice that my good friend Peter Gunther has compiled this selection of F. W. Boreham's writings so that a new generation of readers may get acquainted with this remarkable man. Boreham's critics (and every successful preacher has them) called his sermons "homiletical confectionery" because he didn't follow the usual analytical treatment of a text. But Boreham was successful because he avoided theological jargon and rigid homiletical outlines. He got straight to the heart of a passage of Scripture and then imaginatively applied the truth to the hearts of his listeners.

If you are already addicted to Boreham, this volume will surely warm your heart. If you are not yet acquainted with this remarkable preacher — and Boreham always considered himself a preacher first and a writer second — then you are in for a great treat. I'm sure that this collection will whet your appetite for more, and that you will join the growing host of appreciative readers who are constantly searching out new Boreham titles to add to their library. Happy reading — and happy hunting!

WARREN W. WIERSBE
Associate Teacher
"Back to the Bible Broadcast"
Lincoln, Nebraska

Preface

When I introduce my fellow-Australian F. W. Boreham as one of the stars students should study in the *History of Preaching* course here at Golden Gate Baptist Theological Seminary, they tolerate him mostly as an idiosyncratic excess of their professor's own South Pacific genesis. His move to favoritism among many other giants is very swift, however, for most of them.

Australian Baptists are naturally proud of the only preacher among them who has gained such international eminence and literary excellence. But he belongs not to Australians alone, nor to New Zealanders, nor to the British, all of whom may lay some claim to a share in his fame. He belongs to the whole world and to the whole evangelical church. Wherever thinking, feeling, and believing Christians live — there Boreham's words remain relevant. His insight, perspicacity, and erudition remain unequaled. His incisive application of the lessons of history and literature as applied to spiritual living and his dynamic relation of these to biblical truths still outshine most others.

You and I live in a generation where Boreham is largely forgotten. This fine selection of his writings will do much now to fill such a gap.

When Billy Graham visited England, the man he wanted above all to meet was the saintly Dr. W. E. Sangster. In Melbourne, Australia, his choice was the encouraging Dr. F. W. Boreham. After recounting memories of D. L. Moody for Mr. Graham, Boreham had both of his visitors kneel while "with face uplifted to heaven and his hands on our heads he poured out his great heart in a consecrating prayer which will follow us through the years like the sound of a great Amen."*

In this volume many will relate to Frank Boreham so as to hear words and discover thoughts that will become just such an abiding benediction.

If you are a preacher you will discover sermon ideas sprouting like spring wheat from every page. If you are a reader you will savor thoughts expressed in words of such finesse that their quality stands almost unique. If you are Christ's your heart will quicken, your mind will stretch, and your tongue will move to praise Him.

That says a lot for the *book*. It says more about the *writer*. It says *most* about the reality of his thoughts and themes.

> CRAIG P. SKINNER
> Professor of Preaching
> Golden Gate Baptist Theological Seminary
> Mill Valley, California

* F. W. Boreham, *The Last Milestone*, Introduction (London: Epworth, 1961), p. 20.

1

MARTIN LUTHER

(1483-1546)

Martin Luther led the Protestant Reformation and made an important contribution to German literature with his translation of the Bible. He wrote more than four hundred works, from pamphlets to large books. He arranged a new order of church services as well as a new system of church government. He wrote catechisms for the common people and introduced singing by the congregation. Of the 125 hymns that he wrote, the best known is "Ein Feste Burg" ("A Mighty Fortress").

His text: "The just shall live by his faith" (Habakkuk 2:4).

I

It goes without saying that the text that made Martin Luther made history with a vengeance.

When, through its mystical but mighty ministry, Martin Luther entered into newness of life, the face of the world was changed. It was as though all the windows of Europe had been suddenly thrown open, and the sunshine came streaming in everywhere. The destinies of empires were turned that day into a new channel. Carlyle has a stirring and dramatic chapter in which he shows that every nation under heaven stood or fell according to the attitude that it assumed towards Martin Luther. "I call this Luther a true Great Man," he exclaims. "He is great in intellect, great in courage, great in affection and integrity; one of our most lovable and gracious men. He is great, not as a hewn obelisk is great, but as an Alpine mountain is great; so simple, honest, spontaneous; not setting himself up to be great, but there for quite another purpose than the purpose of being great!" "A mighty man," he says again; "what were all emperors, popes and potentates in comparison? His light was to flame as a beacon over long centuries and epochs of the world; the whole world and its history was waiting for this man!" And elsewhere he declares that the moment in which Luther defied the wrath of the Diet of Worms was the greatest moment in the modern history of men. Here, then, was "the man"; what was "the text" that made him?

II

Let us visit a couple of very interesting European libraries! And here, in the Convent Library at Erfurt, we are shown an exceedingly famous and beautiful picture. It represents Luther as a young monk of four and twenty, poring in the early morning over a copy of the Scriptures to which a bit of broken chain is hanging. The dawn is stealing through the open lattice, illumining both the open Bible and the eager face of its reader. And on the page that the young monk so intently studies are to be seen the words: "The just shall live by faith."

"The just shall live by faith!"

"The just shall live by faith!"

These, then, are the words that made the world all over again. And now, leaving the Convent Library at Erfurt, let us visit another library, the Library of Rudolstadt! For here, in a glass case, we shall discover a manuscript that will fascinate us. It is a letter in the handwriting of Dr. Paul Luther, the reformer's youngest son. "In the year 1544," we read, "my late dearest father, in the presence of us all, narrated the whole story of his journey to Rome. He acknowledged with great joy that, in that city, through the Spirit of Jesus Christ, he had come to the knowledge of the truth of the everlasting gospel. It happened in this way. As he repeated his prayers on the Lateran staircase, the words of the Prophet Habakkuk came suddenly to his mind: 'The just shall live by faith.' Thereupon he ceased his prayers, returned to Wittenberg, and took this as the chief foundation of all his doctrine."

"The just shall live by faith!"

"The just shall live by faith!"

The picture in the one library, and the manuscript in the other, have told us all that we desire to know.

III

"The just shall live by faith!"

"The just shall live by faith!"

The words do not flash or glitter. Like the ocean, they do not give any indication upon the surface of the profundities and mysteries that lie concealed beneath. And yet of what other text can it be said that, occurring in the Old Testament, it is thrice quoted in the New?

"The just shall live by faith!" cries the Prophet.

"The just shall live by faith!" says Paul, when he addresses a letter to the greatest of the European churches [Romans 1:17].

"The just shall live by faith!" he says again, in his letter to the greatest of the Asiatic churches [Galatians 3:11].

"The just shall live by faith!" says the writer of the epistle to the Hebrews, addressing himself to Jews [Hebrews 10:38].

It is as though it were the sum and substance of everything, to be proclaimed by prophets in the old dispensation, and echoed by apostles in the new; to be translated into all languages and transmitted to every section of the habitable earth. Indeed, Bishop Lightfoot as good as says that the words represent the concentration and epitome of all revealed religion. "The whole law," he says, "was given to Moses in six hundred and thirteen precepts. David, in the fifteenth Psalm, brings them all within the compass of eleven. Isaiah reduces them to six; Micah to three; and Isaiah, in a later passage, to two. But Habakkuk condenses them all into one: 'The just shall live by faith!'"

And this string of monosyllables that sums up everything and is sent to everybody — the old world's text, the new world's text, the prophet's text, the Jew's text, the European's text, the Asiatic's text, everybody's text — is, in a special and peculiar sense, Martin Luther's text. We made that discovery in the libraries of Erfurt and Rudolstadt; and we shall, as we proceed, find abundant evidence to confirm us in that conclusion.

IV

For, strangely enough, the text that echoed itself three times in the New Testament, echoed itself three times also in the experience of Luther. It met him at Wittenberg, it met him at Bologna, and it finally mastered him at Rome.

It was at Wittenberg that the incident occurred which we have already seen transferred to the painter's canvas. In the retirement of his quiet cell, whilst the world is still wrapped in slumber, he pores over the epistle to the Romans. Paul's quotation from Habakkuk strangely captivates him.

"The just shall live by faith!"

"The just shall live by faith!"

"This precept," says the historian, "fascinates him. 'For the just, then,' he says to himself, 'there is a life different from that of other men; and this life is the gift of faith!' This promise, to which he opens all his heart, as if God had placed it there specially for him, unveils to him the mystery of the Christian life. For years afterwards, in the midst of his numerous occupations, he fancies that he still hears the words repeating themselves to him over and over again."

"The just shall live by faith!"

"The just shall live by faith!"

Years pass. Luther travels. In the course of his journey, he crosses the Alps, is entertained at a Benedictine Convent at Bologna, and is there overtaken by a serious sickness. His mind relapses into utmost darkness and dejection. To die thus, under a burning sky and in a foreign land! He shudders at the thought. "The sense of his sinfulness troubles him; the prospect of judgment fills him with dread. But at the very moment at which these terrors reach their highest pitch, the words that had already struck him at Wittenberg recur forcibly to his memory and enlighten his soul like a ray from heaven —

'The just shall live by faith!'

'The just shall live by faith!'

"Thus restored and comforted," the record concludes, "he soon regains his health and resumes his journey."

The third of these experiences — the experience narrated in that fireside conversation of which the manuscript at Rudolstadt has told us — befalls him at Rome. "Wishing to obtain an indulgence promised by the Pope to all who shall ascend Pilate's Staircase on their knees, the good Saxon monk is painfully creeping up those steps which, he is told, were miraculously transported from Jerusalem to Rome. Whilst he is performing this meritorious act, however, he thinks he hears a voice of thunder crying, as at Wittenberg and Bologna —

'The just shall live by faith!'

'The just shall live by faith!'

"These words, that twice before have struck him like the voice of an angel from heaven, resound unceasingly and powerfully within him. He rises in amazement from the steps up which he is dragging his body; he shudders at himself; he is ashamed at seeing to what a depth superstition has plunged him. He flies far from the scene of his folly."

Thus, thrice in the New Testament and thrice in the life of Luther, the text speaks with singular appropriateness and effect.

V

"This powerful text," remarks Merle D' Aubigné, "has a mysterious influence on the life of Luther. It was a 'creative sentence,' both for the reformer and for the Reformation. It was in these words that God then said, 'Let there be light!' and there was light!"

VI

It was the unveiling of the Face of God! Until this great transforming text flashed its light into the soul of Luther, his thought of God was a pagan thought. And the pagan thought is an unjust thought, an unworthy thought, a cruel thought. Look at this Indian devotee! From head to foot he bears the marks of the torture that he has inflicted upon his body in his frantic efforts to give pleasure to his god. His back is a tangle of scars. The flesh has been lacerated by the pitiless hooks by which he has swung himself on the terrible churuka. Iron spears have been repeatedly run through his tongue. His ears are torn to ribbons. What does it mean? It can only mean that he worships a fiend! His god loves to see him in anguish! His cries of pain are music in the ears of the deity whom he adores! This ceaseless orgy of torture is his futile endeavour to satisfy the idol's lust for blood. Luther made precisely the same mistake. To his sensitive mind, every thought of God was a thing of terror. "When I was young," he tells us, "it happened that at Eisleben, on Corpus Christi day, I was walking with the procession, when, suddenly, the sight of the Holy Sacrament, which was carried by Doctor Staupitz, so terrified me that a cold sweat covered my body and I believed myself dying of terror." All through his convent days he proceeds upon the assumption that God gloats over his misery. His life is a longdrawn-out agony. He creeps like a shadow along the galleries of the cloister, the walls echoing with his dismal moanings. His body wastes to a skeleton; his strength ebbs away: on more than one occasion his brother monks find him prostrate on the convent floor and pick him up for dead. And all the time he thinks of God as One who can find delight in these continuous torments! The just shall live, he says to himself, by penance and by pain. The just shall live by fasting; the just shall live by fear.

VII

"The just shall live by fear!" Luther mutters to himself every day of his life.

"The just shall live by faith!" says the text that breaks upon him like a light from heaven.

"By fear! By fear!"

"By faith! By faith!"

And what is faith? The theologians may find difficulty in defining it, yet every little child knows what it is. In all the days of my own ministry I have found only one definition that has satisfied me, and whenever I have had occasion to speak of faith, I have recited it. It is Bishop O'Brien's:

"They who know what is meant by faith in a promise, know what is meant by faith in the gospel; they who know what is meant by faith in a remedy, know what is meant by faith in the blood of the Redeemer; they who know what is meant by faith in a physician, faith in an advocate, faith in a friend, know, too, what is meant by faith in the Lord Jesus Christ."

With the coming of the text, Luther passes from the realm of "fear" into the realm of "faith." It is like passing from the rigors of an arctic night into the sunshine of a summer day; it is like passing from a crowded city slum into the fields where the daffodils dance and linnets sing; it is like passing into a new world; it is like "entering Paradise!"

VIII

Yes, it is like "entering Paradise!" The expression is his, not mine. "Before those words broke upon my mind," he says, "I hated God and was angry with Him because, not content with frightening us sinners by the law and by the miseries of life, He still further increased our torture by the gospel. But when, by the Spirit of God, I understood these words —

'The just shall live by faith!'

'The just shall live by faith!'

— then I felt born again like a new man; I entered through the open doors into 'the very Paradise of God!'"

"Henceforward," he says again, "I saw the beloved and holy Scriptures with other eyes. The words that I had previously detested, I began from that hour to value and to love as the sweetest and most consoling words in the Bible. In very truth, this text was to me 'the true gate of Paradise!'"

"An open door into the very Paradise of God!"

"This text was to me the true gate of Paradise!"

And they who enter into the City of God by that gate will go no more out forever.

2

HUGH LATIMER
(1485-1555)

Hugh Latimer was a martyr of the Protestant Reformation in England. He studied at Cambridge University and became a priest, named chaplain of King Henry VIII. Later he became bishop of Worcester. He refused to sign the king's six articles, which he believed represented a return of England to Catholicism, and as a result was confined to the Tower of London and later imprisoned there by Queen Mary. He and Nicholas Ridley were burned at the stake along with nearly 300 other Protestant leaders under Queen Mary.

His text: "This is a faithful saying, and worthy of all acceptation, that Christ Jesus came into the world to save sinners; of whom I am chief" (1 Timothy 1:15).

I

There is excitement in the streets of London! Who is this upon whom the crowd is pressing as he passes down the Strand? Women throw open the windows and gaze admiringly out; shopkeepers rush from behind their counters to join the throng as it approaches; apprentices fling aside their tools and, from every lane and alley, pour into the street; waggoners rein in their horses and leave them for a moment unattended; the taverns empty as the procession draws near them! Everybody is anxious to catch a glimpse of this man's face; to hear, if possible, the sound of his voice; or, better still, to clasp his hand as he passes. For this is Hugh Latimer; the terror of evil-doers; the idol of the

9

common people; and, to use the phraseology of a chronicler of the period, "the honestest man in England." By sheer force of character he has raised himself from a ploughman's cottage to a bishop's palace — an achievement that, in the sixteenth century, stands without precedent or parallel. "My father was a yeoman," he says, in the course of a sermon preached before the King, "my father was a yeoman, and had no lands of his own; he had a farm of three or four pounds a year at the utmost, and thereupon he tilled so much as kept half-a-dozen men. He had walk for a hundred sheep; and my mother milked thirty kine. He kept me at school, or else I had not been able to have preached before the King's majesty now."

Nor has his elevation spoiled him. He has borne with him in his exaltations the spirit of the common people. He feels as they feel; he thinks as they think; he even speaks as they speak. It was said of him, as of his Master, that the common people heard him gladly. In cathedral pulpits and royal chapels he speaks a dialect that the common people can readily understand; he uses homely illustrations gathered from the farm, the kitchen, and the counting house; he studiously eschews the pedantries of the schoolmen and the subtleties of the theologians. His sermons are, as Macaulay says, "the plain talk of a plain man, who sprang from the body of the people, who sympathized strongly with their wants and their feelings, and who boldly uttered their opinions."

It was on account of the fearless way in which stout-hearted old Hugh exposed the misdeeds of men in ermine tippets and gold collars that the Londoners cheered him as he walked down the Strand to preach at Whitehall, struggled for a touch of his gown, and bawled, "Have at them, Father Latimer!"

There he goes, then; a man of sound sense, honest affection, earnest purpose and sturdy speech; a man whose pale face, stooping figure, and emaciated frame show that it has cost him something to struggle upwards from the ploughshare to the palace; a man who looks for all the world like some old Hebrew prophet transplanted incongruously into the prosaic life of London! He passes down the Strand with the people surging fondly around him. He loves the people, and is pleased with their confidence in him. His heart is simple enough and human enough to find the sweetest of all music in the plaudits that are ringing in his ears. So much for London; we must go to Oxford!

II

There is excitement in the streets of Oxford! Who is this upon whom the crowd is pressing as he passes down from the mayor's house to the open ground in front of Balliol College? Again, women are leaning out of the windows; shopkeepers are forsaking their counters; apprentices are throwing aside their tools; and drivers are deserting their horses that they may stare at him. It is Hugh Latimer again! He is a little thinner than when we saw him in London; for he has exchanged a palace for a prison. The people still press upon him and make progress difficult; but this time they crowd around him that they may curse him! It is the old story of "Hosannah!" one day and "Away with Him! Crucify Him!" the next. The multitude is a fickle master. Since we saw him in the Strand, the crown has passed from one head to another; the court has changed its ways to gratify the whims of its new mistress; the Government has swung round to match the moods of the court; and the people, like sheep, have followed their leaders. They are prepared now to crown the men whom before they would have crucified, and to crucify the men whom they would then have crowned. But Hugh Latimer and his companion — for this time he is not alone — are not of the same accommodating temper. Hugh Latimer is still "the honestest man in England!" His conscience is still his only monitor; his tongue is still free; his soul is not for sale! And so —

In Oxford town the faggots they piled,
With furious haste and with curses wild,
Round two brave men of our British breed,
Who dared to stand true to their speech and deed;
Round two brave men of that sturdy race,
Who with tremorless souls the worst can face;
Round two brave souls who could keep their tryst
Through a pathway of fire to follow Christ.
And the flames leaped up, but the blinding smoke
Could not the soul of Hugh Latimer choke;
For, said he, "Brother Ridley, be of good cheer,
A candle in England is lighted here,
Which by grace of God shall never go out!" -
And that speech in whispers was echoed about -
Latimer's Light shall never go out,
However the winds may blow it about.
Latimer's Light has come to stay
Till the trump of a coming judging day.

"Bishop Ridley," so runs the record, "first entered the lists, dressed in his episcopal habit; and, soon after, Bishop Latimer, dressed, as usual, in his prison garb. Master Latimer now suffered the keeper to pull off his prison garb and then he appeared in his shroud. Being ready, he fervently recommended his soul to God, and then he delivered himself to the executioner, saying to the Bishop of London these prophetical words: 'We shall this day, my lord, light such a candle in England as shall never be extinguished!'"

But it is time that we went back forty years or so, to a time long before either of the processions that we have just witnessed took place. We must ascertain at what flame the light that kindled that candle was itself ignited.

III

Very early in the sixteenth century, England was visited by one of the greatest scholars of the Renaissance, Desiderius Erasmus. After being welcomed with open arms at the Universities, he returned to the Continent and engrossed himself in his learned researches. At Cambridge, however, he had made a profound and indelible impression on at least one of the scholars. Thomas Bilney, familiarly known as "Little Bilney," was feeling, in a vague and indefinite way, the emptiness of the religion that he had been taught. He felt that Erasmus possessed a secret that was hidden from English eyes, and he vowed that, whatever it might cost him, he would purchase every line that came from the great master's pen. In France, Erasmus translated the New Testament into Latin. The ingenuity and industry of Bilney soon secured for him a copy of the book. As to its effect upon him, he shall speak for himself. "My soul was sick," he says, "and I longed for peace, but nowhere could I find it. I went to the priests, and they appointed my pennances and pilgrimages; yet by these things my poor sick soul was nothing profited. But at last I heard of Jesus. It was then, when first the New Testament was set forth by Erasmus, that the light came. I bought the book, being drawn thereto rather by the Latin than by the Word of God, for at that time I knew not what the Word of God meant. And, on the first reading of it, as I well remember, I chanced upon these words, 'This is a faithful saying, and worthy of all acceptation, that Christ Jesus came into the world to save sinners, of whom I am chief.' That one sentence, through God's inward working, did so lift up my poor bruised spirit that the very bones within me leaped for joy and gladness. It was as if, after a long, dark night, day had suddenly broke!" But what has all this to do with Hugh Latimer?

IV

In those days Latimer was preaching at Cambridge, and all who heard him fell under the spell of his transparent honesty and rugged eloquence. Latimer was then the sturdy champion of the old religion and the uncompromising foe of all who were endeavoring to introduce the new learning. Of all the friars, he was the most punctilious, the most zealous, the most devoted. Bilney went to hear him and fell in love with him at once. He saw that the preacher was mistaken; that his eyes had not been opened to the sublimities that had flooded his own soul with gladness; but he recognized his sincerity, his earnestness, and his resistless power; and he longed to be the instrument of his illumination. If only he could do for Latimer what Aquila and Priscilla did for Apollos, and expound unto him the way of God more perfectly! It became the dream and desire of Bilney's life. "O God," he cried, "I am but 'Little Bilney,' and shall never do any great thing for Thee; but give me the soul of that man, Hugh Latimer, and what wonders *he* shall do in Thy most holy Name!"

Where there's a will there's a way! One day, as Latimer descends from the pulpit, he passes so close to Bilney that his robes almost brush the student's face. Like a flash, a sudden inspiration leaps to Bilney's mind. "Prithee, Father Latimer," he whispers, "may I confess my soul to thee?" The preacher beckons, and, into the quiet room adjoining, the student follows.

Of all the strange stories that heartbroken penitents have poured into the ears of Father-confessors since first the confessional was established, *that* was the strangest! Bilney falls on his knees at Latimer's feet and allows his soul, pent up for so long, to utter itself freely at last. He tells of the aching hunger of his heart; he tells of the visit of Erasmus; he tells of the purchase of the book; and then he tells of the text. "There it stood," he says, the tears standing in his eyes, "the very word I wanted. It seemed to be written in letters of light: 'This is a faithful saying, and worthy of all acceptation, that Christ Jesus came into the world to save sinners.' O Father Latimer," he cries, the passion of his fervor increasing as the memory of his own experience rushes back upon him, "I went to the priests and they pointed me to broken cisterns that held no water and only mocked my thirst! I bore the load of my sins until my soul was crushed beneath the burden! And then I saw that 'Christ Jesus came into the world to save sinners; of whom I am chief'; and now, being justified by faith, I have peace with God through our Lord Jesus Christ!"

Latimer is taken by storm. He is completely overwhelmed. He, too, knows the aching dissatisfaction that Bilney has described. He has experienced for years the same insatiable hunger, the same devouring thirst. To the astonishment of Bilney, Latimer rises and then kneels beside him. The Father-confessor seeks guidance from his penitent! Bilney draws from his pocket the sacred volume that has brought such comfort and such rapture to his own soul. It falls open at the passage that Bilney has read to himself over and over again: "This is a faithful saying, and worthy of all acceptation, that Christ Jesus came into the world to save sinners; of whom I am chief." The light that never was on sea or shore illumines the soul of Hugh Latimer, and Bilney sees that the passionate desire of his heart has been granted him. And from that hour Bilney and Latimer lived only that they might unfold to all kinds and conditions of men the unsearchable riches of Christ.

V

"This is a faithful saying!" That is the preacher's comfort. In the course of a recent tour through Western Australia, I was taken through the gold diggings. And, near Kanowna, I was shown the spot on which, years ago, there gathered one of the largest and most extraordinary congregations that ever assembled on this side of the world. It was whispered all over the diggings that an enormous nugget had been found and that Father Long, the local priest, had seen it and knew exactly where it was discovered. Morning, noon, and night the young priest was pestered by eager gold-hunters for information; but to one and all his lips were sealed. At last he consented to announce publicly the exact locality of the wonderful find. At the hour fixed men came from far and near, some on horseback, some on camels, some in all kinds of conveyances, and thousands on foot. It was the largest gathering of diggers in the history of the gold fields. At the appointed time Father Long appeared, surveyed the great sea of bronzed and bearded faces, and then announced that the "Sacred

Nugget" had been found in the Lake Gwynne country. In a moment the crowd had vanished! There was the wildest stampede for the territory to which the priest had pointed them. But as the days passed by, the disappointed seekers, in twos and threes, came dribbling back. Not a glint of gold had been seen by any of them! And then the truth flashed upon them. The priest had been hoaxed! The "Sacred Nugget" was a mass of common metal splashed with gold paint! Father Long took the matter bitterly to heart; he went to bed a broken and humiliated man; and, a few months later, disconsolate, he died! It was a great day in Hugh Latimer's life when he got among the "faithful sayings," the sayings of which he was certain, the sayings that could never bring to any confiding hearer the heartbreak and disgust of disappointment.

VI

"It is worthy of all acceptation!" It is worthy! It is worthy of *your* acceptance, your Majesty, for this proclamation craves no patronage! It is worthy of *your* acceptance, your Excellency, your Grace, my Lords, Ladies, and Gentlemen all, for the gospel asks no favors! It is worthy, worthy, worthy of the acceptance of you *all!* Hugh Latimer stood before kings and courtiers and declared that "this is a faithful saying, and worthy of all acceptation, that Christ Jesus came into the world to save sinners." Never once did he forget the dignity of his message: it was faithful; it was worthy in its own right of the acceptance of the lordliest; and he himself staked his life upon it at the last!

VII

Dr. Archibald Alexander, of Princeton, was for sixty years a minister of Christ; and for forty of those years he was Professor of Divinity. No man in America was more revered or beloved. He died on October 22, 1851. As he lay dying, he was heard by a friend to say, "All my theology is reduced now to this narrow compass: 'This is a faithful saying, and worthy of all acceptation, that Christ Jesus came into the world to save sinners.'" In life and in death Hugh Latimer was of pretty much the same mind.

3

WILLIAM TYNDALE
(1494-1536)

William Tyndale, a contemporary of Martin Luther, was one of the great leaders of the Protestant Reformation in England. He became very proficient in the Greek language while attending the universities of Oxford and Cambridge, and studied Hebrew in Hamburg, Germany, with some prominent Jews. It was reading the Greek New Testament of Erasmus and the works of Martin Luther that caused him to want to give the Bible to the common people in their own language. He translated the New Testament into English and had it published in Worms, Germany. He also translated the Pentateuch and the book of Jonah. On October 6, 1536, Tyndale was first strangled and then burned at the stake. His last words, spoken in a loud voice, were "Lord, open the king of England's eyes!"

His text: "We love him, because he first loved us" (1 John 4:19).

I

How heartily and incredulously Harry Walsh would have laughed if some little bird had whispered in his ear that, in centuries to come, men would speak of William Tyndale as a grave and austere scholar, a stern and gloomy reformer, a severe and unbending controversialist! And Humphrey Monmouth would have felt very similarly. For Harry Walsh, a sunny little fellow of six, living at Old Sodbury, and Humphrey Monmouth, an alderman and well-known merchant of the city of London, knew Mr. Tyndale as one of the most winsome, one of the most genial, and one of the most lovable of men. Their happiest hours were spent

17

in his society. Harry was the elder son of Sir John Walsh, a knight of Gloucestershire, and Mr. Tyndale was his private tutor. Here they are, sitting together beside a stile under a giant chestnut tree, surveying from this green and graceful hillside the quaint little hamlet nestling in the hollow! Harry, in all the bravery of his trim velvet suit, with silk stockings and silver buckles, is perched on the top of the stile. His tutor, a young man of thirty, of well-knit frame and thoughtful but pleasant face, with nut-brown hair and deep-set hazel eyes, is seated on the footstep below him. A little brown squirrel eyes them suspiciously from a branch overhead, and a cuckoo is calling from the copse near by. Harry carries an armful of bluebells.

"What wonderful times we are living in!" exclaims Mr. Tyndale, his eyes sparkling with enthusiasm. "Why, you and I ought to thank God every day, Harry, that He has sent us into the world just now! Every morning brings news of some fresh wonder!"

It was no exaggeration. The air literally tingled with sensation and romance. It was an age of thrills! The world was being made all over again. Civilization was being overhauled and recast. The very planet was assuming a fresh shape. One day Bartholomew Diaz added Africa to the map of the world; the next, Columbus added America; and then Vasco da Gama unveiled India to the eyes of Europe. Continents were springing up like mushrooms on a misty morning. And fresh continents produced fresh oceans. Twenty years after Columbus sailed across the Atlantic, Nuñez de Balboa

> ... with eagle eyes
> First stared at the Pacific — and all his men
> Looked at each other with a wild surmise —
> Silent, upon a peak in Darien.

Navigation was the fever of the hour. The vast oceans, so long a waste of loneliness, became a snowstorm of white sails. Every few days bronzed explorers seemed to be stepping from the decks of battered and weatherbeaten vessels to tell of new and astonishing discoveries in the Atlantic, in the Pacific, in the Indian Ocean — everywhere.

Nor was the land less sensational than the sea. For one thing, William Caxton was setting up his magic presses. Macaulay says that the invention of printing was the most notable event that took place during a thousand years of human history. It took the world by storm. Learned men, fashionable ladies, and great nobles thronged Caxton's little printing-house to see how the miracle was performed; while less intelligent people declined to go near it, declaring that such results could only be achieved by witchery, necromancy, and illicit commerce with evil spirits.

Moreover, to add to the wonder of it all, the printing-press came into the world at the very moment when the world had something worth printing. For it was the age of the Renaissance and the Reformation! While Columbus was revealing a new world in the West, Copernicus was opening up a new universe in the skies, and Martin Luther was arousing a thousand thunders by tearing down the curtain that intervened between the common people and the Kingdom of Heaven. Faith's pilgrim path was being blazed. Astronomy was being born. Culture of all kinds was exciting boundless enthusiasm. Men were eager to think. In the realms of Religion, of Science, of Philosophy, of Music, of Art — indeed, in every department of learning — illustrious adventurers, whose names will live forever, appeared like bright stars that twinkle suddenly out of the age-long dark. Men fell in love with the world — with this world and with every other. An infinite horizon was opened to the simplest minds. People who had lived in a tiny village found themselves exploring mighty continents. Lecky declares that the enlightenment and civilization of ancient times was restricted almost entirely to great centers like Athens and Rome; it never penetrated rural districts. In the awakening that took place in Tyndale's boyhood and youth it was quite otherwise. Mysteries that had for centuries baffled the minds of sages became the gossip of every chimney-corner and the talk of every taproom.

"What wonderful times we are living in," exclaims Mr. Tyndale, partly to himself and partly to his young charge perched on the rustic stile. Harry's golden hours are the hours that he spends rambling across the fields or through the woods in Mr. Tyndale's delightful company. For he knows that, as soon as they warm to their stride, his tutor will tell him the latest wonder of which the coach from London has brought word.

II

All things come to an end, however, as Harry discovers to his sorrow. As long as he lived he always declared that the deepest shadow that darkened his happy boyhood was his tutor's resignation. He never forgot the evening on which Mr. Tyndale told him that he must leave Old Sodbury.

The candles having been lit, Mr. Tyndale, as is his custom, reads to the two boys — Harry and Richard — a few verses from his Greek Testament, translating and commenting as he goes along.

"We must read our favorite verses tonight," he had said, with a smile of singular sweetness in which, however, a suspicion of sadness seemed to linger. The boys know exactly the passage to which he refers. They know how dear to him are the verses that he has taught them, too, to love.

"'Ye are of God, little children,'" he begins, and reads on till he comes to the words: "We love Him because He first loved us." Those words, he used to tell the boys, were the pearly gate through which he entered the Kingdom.

"I used to think," he said, "that salvation was not for me, since I did not love God; but those precious words showed me that God does not love us because we first loved Him. No, no; 'we love Him because He first loved us.' It makes all the difference!"

The familiar passage having been read once more, Mr. Tyndale tells them that he is leaving them. The boys are soon in tears, and the tutor's voice is husky.

"But why," demands Richard, in a passion of childish grief, "why must you go?"

He draws them to him and attempts to explain.

"I must go," he says quietly, with one arm round the shoulders of each boy, "because I have found the work that God has sent me into the world to do. You have heard the things that have been said at dinner. Great and wise men, even preachers and prelates of the Church, come to dine with your father and mother, and say things that they could not possibly say if they knew aught of the Scriptures. If learned doctors and eloquent preachers are so ignorant of the divine Word, is it any wonder that 'the people' are in darkness? A new day is dawning; the people are reading and thinking; it is time they had the Bible in their own tongue; and so, as I told your father and Dr. Hampton at dinner last night, I have resolved that, if God spare my life, I will cause every ploughboy in England to know the Scriptures better than the priests and prelates know them now. But it cannot be done here. I must go to London, and there, I trust, Bishop Tunstall will counsel and assist me."

And so, after taking a sorrowful farewell of the household at

Old Sodbury, Mr. Tyndale turns his face towards London.

III

But London receives him with a scowl. He soon discovers that he has poked his hand into a hornets' nest. On his first appearance at the palace, the bishop gives him the cold shoulder; and, when he persists in his overtures, he is threatened with all the thunderbolts that the Church can hurl. By every ship that glides up the Thames the writings of Martin Luther are being surreptitiously imported into England, and men are being hurried to prison and to death for reading them. There is nothing to indicate to the disappointed young tutor that, in centuries to come, his statue will hold a place of honor on the Victoria Embankment, and that, at its unveiling, princes and peers will bare their heads in reverence to his illustrious memory!

And yet, while Church and State frown upon his project and eye him with suspicion, those who come into intimate touch with him are captivated by his charm. From his old employer at Sodbury he brings letters of introduction to some of the merchant princes of the metropolis, and in their homes he soon becomes a loved and honored guest. With Alderman Humphrey Monmouth he stayed for more than six months. On weekdays he worked quietly at his translation. "But," as an old chronicler says, "when Sunday came, then went he to some merchant's house or other, whither came many other merchants, and unto them would he read some one parcel of Scripture, the which proceeded so sweetly, gently, and fruitfully from him that it was a heavenly comfort to the audience to hear him read the Scriptures. He particularly loved the writings of St. John."

Harry and Richard Walsh must have smiled knowingly if that last sentence ever came under their notice: "He particularly loved the writings of St. John." They would see again the glowing face of their old tutor as he read the sentences that were so dear to him. And when he came to the words: "We love Him because He first loved us," they would once more hear him tell of the way in which those priceless syllables had first impressed his soul.

Two things, however, are now clear. The first is that the people of England are hungry for the Word of God in their mother tongue; the second is that it is out of the question to attempt a publication in London. This being so, he must brace himself for another painful wrench. Tearing himself from the homes in which so many delightful hours have been spent, he sets sail for the Continent.

IV

And, on the Continent, he knows of at least one kindred spirit. Martin Luther is hard at work translating the Scriptures. "Would to God," Luther cried, "that this book were in every language and in every home!" Mr. Tyndale decides to hasten to Wittenberg and talk things over with the man who was shaking the very foundations of Europe. It is a pity that we have no classical painting of that historic meeting.

Luther and Tyndale! The German Bible of today is the most enduring and most glorious monument to Martin Luther; the English Bible of today is the most enduring and most glorious monument to William Tyndale! And here, in 1524, we see the two men spending a few memorable days together!

The rest of the story is well known. We have all chuckled over the way in which Tyndale outwitted his old antagonist, the Bishop of London. The New Testament in English is at last complete. "It is called the 'New Testament,'" Tyndale explains, "because it is the Last Will of Jesus Christ, in which He bequeaths all His goods to those that repent and believe." But how is it to reach England? The ports are closed against it! The book is contraband! Yet, in crates and casks and cases, in boxes and barrels and bales, in rolls of cloth and sacks of flour and bundles of merchandise, the Testaments come pouring into the country!

"Very well!" retorts the bishop, "if we cannot 'ban' the books, we'll 'buy' the books and 'burn' them!" He does so, only to discover, as soon as the flames of his famous fire have died down, that, in buying them, he has provided Tyndale with the wherewithal to print a larger and better edition!

We have all experienced the thrill of this brave, adventurous career. He was harassed; he was excommunicated; he was driven from pillar to post; he was hunted from country to country; he was shipwrecked; he was betrayed; he was imprisoned; he was tortured; and, at last, he was sentenced to a shameful death.

And we have all felt the pathos of that last letter of his. He is only fifty-six; but he is worn out and decrepit. Lying in his damp cell at Vilvorde, awaiting the stroke that is to emancipate his soul for ever, he reminds his friends that the date of his execution has not been fixed and that winter is coming on. "Bring me," he begs, "a warmer cap, something to patch my leggings, a woolen shirt, and above all, my Hebrew Bible!"

"Above all, my Bible!"

The words are eminently characteristic. He lived for the Bible; he died for the Bible; and he mounted the scaffold knowing that the Bible was being read in every chimney-corner, on every village green, and in every tavern and coffee-house in England.

V

It is a sharp October morning in 1536. The young squire of Old Sodbury — Henry Walsh — sits by his dining-room fire with his hands in his pockets and a far-away look in his eye. His handsome young wife, entering the room, demands the cause of his unwonted abstraction. Drawing her to him, he tells her that news has just reached the village that his dear old tutor, William Tyndale, has been strangled and burned for his faith. Then, gently taking her arm, he leads her across the room, and they stand for a moment in reverent silence before the text upon the wall:

WE LOVE HIM BECAUSE HE FIRST LOVED US

He does not repeat the story; she has heard it from his lips so often.

. . . .

And so our studies complete their circuit. For with this text we began. It was "William Law's Text"; it was "William Tyndale's Text"; it is the text of all those whose hearts have made response to the Love that Aches Hungrily until it is Requited.

4

JOHN KNOX
(1514?-1572) *

John Knox led the Protestant Reformation in Scotland. It was after his close friend George Wishart was burned at the stake that Knox began his career as a reformer. He was forced to serve as a galley slave for the French for nineteen months. When Catholic Queen Mary ascended the throne in 1553, Knox went into exile in Germany and Switzerland, where he became acquainted with John Calvin. The Protestant faith was adopted in Scotland as the state religion in 1560. The Parliament appointed Knox chairman of a committee that produced the *First Scottish Confession of Faith* and the *First Book of Discipline*, intended to be used as standards of faith and government for the Scottish Church.

His text: "And this is life eternal, that they might know thee the only true God, and Jesus Christ, whom thou hast sent" (John 17:3).

I

Some men are not born to die. It is their prerogative to live; they come on purpose. A thousand deaths will not lay them in a grave. No disease from within, no danger from without, can by any means destroy them. They bear upon their faces the stamp of the immortal. In more senses than one, they come into the world for good. Among such deathless men John Knox stands out conspicuously.

---

* Little is known of Knox's early life. While some sources place his birth in 1505, the latest evidence seems to indicate the later date.—

When in Edinburgh it is impossible to believe that John Knox lived four hundred years ago. He is so very much alive today that it seems incredible that he was living even then. The people will show you his grave in the middle of the road, and the meagre epitaph on the flat tombstone will do its feeble best to convince you that his voice has been silent for centuries; but you will sceptically shake your head and move away. For, as you walk about the noble and romantic city, John Knox is everywhere! He is the most ubiquitous man you meet. You come upon him at every street corner. Here is the house in which he dwelt; there is the church in which he preached; at every turn you come upon places that are haunted by him still. The very stones vibrate with the strident accents of his voice; the walls echo to his footsteps.

I was introduced to quite a number of people in Edinburgh; but I blush to confess that I have forgotten them all — *all but John Knox.* It really seems to me, looking back upon that visit, that I met John Knox somewhere or other every five minutes. I could hear the ring of his voice; I could see the flash of his eye; I could feel the impress of his huge and commanding personality. The tomb in the middle of the road notwithstanding, John Knox is indisputably the most virile force in Scotland at this hour. I dare say that, like me, he sometimes catches sight of that tomb in the middle of the road. If so, he laughs — as he could laugh —and strides defiantly on. For John Knox was born in 1514, and, behold, he liveth and abideth forever!

II

John Knox, I say, was born in 1514. In 1514, therefore, Scotland was born again. For the birth of such a man is the regeneration of a nation. Life in Knox was not only immortal; it was contagious. Because of Knox, Carlyle affirms, the people began to live! "In the history of Scotland," says Carlyle, himself a Scotsman, "in the history of Scotland I can find but one epoch: it contains nothing of world-interest at all, but this Reformation by Knox." But surely, surely, the sage is nodding! Has Carlyle forgotten Sir Walter Scott and Robert Burns and all Scotland's noble contribution to literature, to industry, to religion and to life? But Carlyle will not retract or modify a single word. "This that Knox did for his nation," he goes on, "was a resurrection as from death. The people began to live! Scotch literature and thought, Scotch industry; James Watt, David Hume, Walter Scott, Robert Burns:

I find John Knox acting in the heart's core of every one of these persons and phenomena: I find that without him they would not have been."

So much have I said in order to show that, beyond the shadow of a doubt, if a text made John Knox, then that text made history.

III

"Go!" said the old reformer to his wife, as he lay dying, and the words were his last, "Go, read where I cast my first anchor!" She needed no more explicit instructions, for he had told her the story again and again. It is Richard Bannatyne, Knox's serving-man, who has placed the scene on record. "On November 24, 1572," he says, "John Knox departed this life to his eternal rest. Early in the afternoon he said, 'Now, for the last time, I commend my spirit, soul, and body' — pointing upon his three fingers — 'into Thy hands, O Lord!' Thereafter, about five o'clock, he said to his wife, 'Go, read where I cast my first anchor!' She did not need to be told, and so she read the seventeenth of John's evangel." Let us listen as she reads it! *"Thou hast given Him authority over all flesh, that He should give eternal life to as many as Thou hast given Him; and this is life eternal, that they might know Thee, the only true God, and Jesus Christ whom Thou hast sent."*

Here was a strange and striking contrast!

"Eternal Life! Life Eternal!" says the Book.

Now listen to the labored breathing from the bed!

The Bed speaks of Death; the Book speaks of Life Everlasting!

"Life!" the dying man starts as the great cadences fall upon his ear.

"This is Life Eternal, that they might *know Thee!"*

"Life Eternal!"

"It was *there,"* he declares with his last breath, "it was *there* that I cast my first anchor!"

IV

How was that first anchor cast? I have tried to piece the records together. Paul never forgot the day on which he saw Stephen stoned; John Knox never forgot the day on which he saw George Wishart burned. Wishart was a man "of such grace" — so Knox himself tells us — "as before him was never heard within this realm." He was regarded with an awe that was next door to superstition, and with an affection that was almost adoration.

Are we not told that in the days when the plague lay over Scotland, "the people of Dundee saw it approaching from the west in the form of a great black cloud? They fell on their knees and prayed, crying to the cloud to pass them by, but even while they prayed it came nearer. Then they looked around for the most holy man among them, to intervene with God on their behalf. All eyes turned to George Wishart, and he stood up, stretching his arms to the cloud, and prayed, and it rolled back." Out on the borders of the town, however, the pestilence was raging, and Wishart, hastening thither, took up his station on the town wall, preaching to the plague-stricken on the one side of him and to the healthy on the other, and exhibiting such courage and intrepidity in grappling with the awful scourge that he became the idol of the grateful people.

In 1546, however, he was convicted of heresy and burned at the foot of the Castle Wynd, opposite the Castle Gate. When he came near to the fire, Knox tells us, he sat down upon his knees, and repeated aloud some of the most touching petitions from the Psalms. As a sign of forgiveness, he kissed the executioner on the cheek, saying: "Lo, here is a token that I forgive thee. My harte, do thine office!" The faggots were kindled, and the leaping flames bore the soul of Wishart triumphantly skywards.

V

And there, a few yards off, stands Knox! Have a good look at him! He is a man "rather under middle height, with broad shoulders, swarthy face, black hair, and a beard of the same color a span and a half long. He has heavy eyebrows, eyes deeply sunk, cheekbones prominent, and cheeks ruddy. The mouth is large, the lips full, especially the upper one. The whole aspect of the man is not unpleasing; and, in moments of emotion, it is invested with an air of dignity and majesty." Knox could never shake from his sensitive mind the tragic yet triumphant scene near the Castle Gate; and when, many years afterwards, he himself turned aside to die, he repeated with closed eyes the prayers that he had heard George Wishart offer under the shadow of the stake.

Was it *then*, I wonder, that John Knox turned sadly homeward and read to himself the great High-priestly prayer in "the seven-teenth of John's evangel?" Was it on that memorable night that he caught a glimpse of the place which all the redeemed hold in the heart of the Redeemer? Was it on that melancholy evening that there broke upon him the revelation of a love that enfolded not only his martyred friend and himself, but the faithful of every time and of every clime? Was it *then* that he opened his heart to the magic and the music of those tremendous words: *"Thou hast given Him authority over all flesh, that He should give eternal life to as many as Thou hast given Him; and this is life eternal, that they might know Thee, the only true God, and Jesus Christ whom Thou hast sent."*

Was it *then?* I cannot say for certain. I only know that we never meet with Knox in Scottish story until after the martyr-dom of Wishart; and I know that, by the events of that sad and tragic day, all his soul was stirred within him. But, although I do not know for certain that the anchor was first cast *then,* I know that it was first cast *there.* "Go!" he said, with the huskiness of death upon his speech, "read me where I cast my first anchor!" And his wife straightway read to him the stately sentences I have just rewritten.

"Life Eternal!"

"This is Life Eternal!"

"This is Life Eternal, that they might *know Thee!"*

"It was there, *there,* THERE, that I cast my first anchor!*"*

VI

Fierce as were the storms that beat upon Knox during the historic years that followed, that anchor bravely held. To say nothing of his experiences at Court and the powerful efforts to coax or cow him into submission, think of those twelve years of exile, nineteen months of which were spent on the French gal-leys. We catch two furtive glimpses of him. The galley in which he is chained makes a cruise round the Scottish coast. It passes so near to the fair fields of Fife that Knox can distinctly see the spires of St. Andrews. At the moment, Knox was so ill that his life was despaired of; and the taunting vision might well have broken his spirit altogether. But the anchor held; the anchor held! "Ah!" exclaimed Knox, raising himself on his elbow, "I see the steeple of that place where God first in public opened my mouth to His glory; and I am fully persuaded, how weak soever I now appear, that I shall not depart this life till that my tongue shall glorify His godly name in the same place."

Again, as Carlyle tells, "a priest one day presented to the galley-slaves an image of the Virgin Mother, requiring that they, the blasphemous heretics, should do it reverence. 'Mother? Mother of God?' said Knox, when the turn came to him, 'This is no Mother of God; this is a piece of painted wood! She is better for swimming, I think, than for being worshiped!' and he flung the thing into the river." Knox had cast his anchor in the seventeenth of John's evangel.

"This is life eternal, that they might know *Thee!*"

And since he had himself found life eternal in the personal friendship of a Personal Redeemer, it was intolerable to him that others should gaze with superstitious eyes on "a bit of painted wood."

The thing fell into the river with a splash. It was a rude jest, but an expressive one. All the Reformation was summed up in it. Eternal life was not to be found in such things. "*This* is life eternal, that they might know Thee." That, says Knox, is where I cast my first anchor; and, through all the storm and stress of those baffling and eventful years, that anchor held!

VII

Nor was there any parting of the cable or dragging of the anchor at the last. Richard Bannatyne, sitting beside his honored master's deathbed, heard a long, long sigh. A singular fancy overtook him.

"Now, sir," he said, "the time to end your battle has come. Remember those comfortable promises of our Savior Jesus Christ which you have so often shown to us. And it may be that, when your eyes are blind and your ears deaf to every other sight and sound, you will still be able to recognize my voice. I shall bend over you and ask if you have still the hope of glory. Will you promise that, if you are able to give me some signal, you will do so?"

The sick man promised, and, soon after, this is what happened:

> Grim in his deep death-anguish the stern old champion lay,
> And the locks upon his pillow were floating thin and grey,
> And, visionless and voiceless, with quick and laboring breath,
> He waited for his exit through life's dark portal, Death.

"Hast thou the hope of glory?" They bowed to catch the thrill
That through some languid token might be responsive still,
Nor watched they long nor waited for some obscure reply,
    He raised a clay-cold finger, and pointed to the sky.

So the death-angel found him, what time his bow he bent,
    To give the struggling spirit a sweet enfranchisement.
So the death-angel left him, what time earth's bonds were riven,
    The cold, stark, stiffening finger still pointing up to heaven.

"He had a sore fight of an existence," says Carlyle, "wrestling with Popes and Principalities; in defeat, contention, life-long struggle; rowing as a galley-slave, wandering as an exile. A sore fight: but he won it! 'Have you hope?' they asked him in his last moment, when he could no longer speak. He lifted his finger, pointed upward, and so died! Honor to him! His works have not died. The letter of his work dies, as of all men's; but the spirit of it, never."

Did I not say in my opening sentences that John Knox is among the immortal humans? When he entered the world, he came into it for good.

VIII

"*This* is life eternal, that they might *know Thee!*" "That," says Knox, with his dying breath, "that is where I cast my first anchor!" It is a sure anchorage, O heart of mine! Cast thine anchor there! Cast thine anchor in the oaths and covenants of the Most High! Cast thine anchor in His infallible, immutable, unbreakable Word! Cast thine anchor in the infinite love of God! Cast thine anchor in the redeeming grace of Christ! Cast thine anchor in the everlasting Gospel! Cast thine anchor in the individual concern of the individual Savior for the individual soul! Cast thine anchor there; and, come what may, that anchor will always hold!

5

OLIVER CROMWELL

(1599-1658)

Oliver Cromwell, a country gentleman and sometimes called
the "uncrowned king," was one of England's greatest soldiers
and statesmen. He apparently did not become a Christian until
he was twenty-four years of age. He adopted the Calvinistic faith
and became known in Parliament as a somewhat uncouth Puritan. Early in public life he launched an attack on the bishops. He
believed that a Christian could establish direct contact with God
through prayer, and that Christian congregations ought to be
allowed to choose their own ministers who should serve them by
preaching and extemporaneous prayer.

Cromwell became Lord Protector of the republican Com-
monwealth of England, Scotland, and Ireland from 1653 to 1658.
Historians regard him as one who contributed to religious tolera-
tion. He strongly opposed severe punishment for minor crimes.
Murder, treason, and rebellion alone were subject to capital
punishment.

Cromwell was buried in Westminster Abbey, but when Charles
II was restored to the throne, his body was hanged and then
buried beneath the gallows. A statue of Oliver Cromwell was
erected in Westminster in 1899.

His text: "I can do all things through Christ which strengtheneth me" (Philippians 4:13).

I

Oliver Cromwell ranks among the giants. Mr. Frederic Harrison

sets his name among the four greatest that England has produced. Carlyle's guffaw upon hearing this pretty piece of patronage would have sounded like a thunderclap! Four, indeed!
Carlyle would say that the other three would look like a trio of
travelling dwarfs grouped about a colossus when they found
themselves in the company of Oliver Cromwell. Carlyle can see
nothing in England's history, nor in any other, more impressive
than the spectacle of this young farmer leaving his fields in Huntingdonshire, putting his plough in the shed, and setting out for
London to hurl the king from his throne, to dismiss the Parliament, and to reconstitute the country on a new and better basis.
He was the one Strong Man; so much stronger than all other men
that he bent them to his will and dominated the entire situation.

Cromwell made history wholesale. How? That is the question
— *How?* And what if, in our search for an answer to that perti-
nent question, we discover that it was by means of *a text?* Let us
go into the matter.

II

My suspicions in this direction were first aroused by reading a
letter that Cromwell wrote to his cousin, Mrs. St. John, before his
public career had begun. In this letter he refers to himself as "a
poor creature." "I am sure," he says, "that I shall never earn the
least mite." Here is strange language for a man who, confident of
his resistless strength, will soon be overturning thrones and tossing crowns and kingdoms hither and thither at his pleasure! Is
there nothing else in the letter that may help us to elucidate the
mystery? There is!

He goes on to tell his cousin that, after all, he does not entirely
despair of himself. Just one ray of hope has shone upon him, one
star has illumined the blackness of his sky. *"One beam in a dark
place,"* he says, *"hath much refreshment in it!"* He does not tell
his cousin what that ray of hope is; he does not name that solitary star; he does not go into particulars as to that "one beam in a
dark place." But we, for our part, must prosecute our investiga-
tions until we have discovered it.

III

It is sometimes best to start at the end of a thing and to work
backwards to the beginning. We will adopt that plan in this

instance. One who was present at the closing scene has graphically described it for us. "At Hampton Court," he says, "being sick nigh unto death, and in his bedchamber, Cromwell called for his Bible and desired an honorable and godly person to read unto him that passage in the fourth of Philippians which saith, *'I can do all things through Christ that strengtheneth me.'* Which read, he observed, 'This scripture did once save my life, when my eldest son, poor Robert, died, which went as a dagger to my heart, indeed it did!' "

This does not tell us much; but it sets our feet in the path that may lead to more. And at any rate it makes clear to us what that "one beam" was that so often had much refreshment in it. *"I can do all things through Christ that strengtheneth me."*

IV

Groping our way back across the years by the aid of the hint given us in those dying words, we come upon that dark and tragic day, nineteen years earlier, when the "son of good promise" died. Unfortunately, the exact circumstances attending the death of the young man have never been recorded. Perhaps the father was too full of grief and bitterness to write for us that sad and tragic tale. All that we know is what he told us on his deathbed. He says that "it went like a dagger to my heart, indeed it did"; and he says that it brought to his aid the text — the "one beam in a dark place" — that saved his life. It was not the first time, as we shall see, that that animating and arousing word had come, like a relieving army entering a beleaguered city, to his deliverance.

But the pathos of that heart-breaking yet heart-healing experience impressed itself indelibly upon his memory; the tale was written in tears; it rushed back upon him as he lay dying; and very often, in the years that lay between his son's death and his own, he feelingly referred to it. In July 1644, for example, I find him writing a letter of sympathy to Colonel Valentine Walton, whose son had also fallen on the field of battle. And in this noble yet tender epistle, Cromwell endeavours to lead the stricken father to the fountains of consolation at which he has slaked his own burning thirst. "Sir," he says, "God hath taken away your eldest son by a cannon-shot. You know my own trials this way, but the Lord supported me. I remembered that my boy had entered into the happiness we all pant for and live for. There, too,

is your precious child, full of glory, never to know sin or sorrow
any more. He was a gallant young man, exceedingly gracious.
God give you His comfort! *You may do all things through Christ
that strengtheneth us.* Seek that, and you shall easily bear your
trial. The Lord be your strength!"

"I can do all things through Christ that strengtheneth me!"
"This scripture," he says, as he lies upon his deathbed, *"did
once save my life!"*
"Seek that!" he says to Colonel Walton, *"seek that! seek that!"*

V

But we must go back farther yet. We are tracing the stream,
but we have not reached the fountain-head. That deathbed testimony at Hampton Court was delivered in 1658. It was in 1639,
or thereabouts, that young Robert, his eldest son, was lying dead.
On each of these occasions the text wonderfully supported him.
But, in each case, it came to him as an old friend and not as a
new acquaintance. For it was in 1638 — the year before Robert's
death and twenty years before the father's — that Cromwell
wrote to his cousin, Mrs. St. John, about the "one beam in a dark
place that hath such exceedingly great refreshment in it." When,
then, did that beam break upon his darksome path for the first
time?
Carlyle thinks that it was in 1623. Cromwell was then in his
twenty-fourth year, with all his life before him. But we may as
well let Carlyle speak for himself. "At about this time took place,"
he says, "what Cromwell, with unspeakable joy, would name his
conversion. Certainly a grand epoch for a man; properly the one
epoch; the turning-point which guides upwards, or guides down-
wards, him and his activities for evermore! Wilt thou join with
the Dragons; wilt thou join with the Gods? Oliver was henceforth
a Christian man; believed in God, not on Sundays only, but on all
days, in all places, and in all cases."
In 1623 it was, then: but how? Piecing the scraps together, a
mere hint there and a vague suggestion there, I gather that it was
somewhat in this way. In 1623 all things were rushing pell-mell
towards turgid crisis, wild tumult and red revolution. At home
and abroad the outlook was as black as could be. The world
wanted a man, a good man, a great man, a strong man, to save it.
Everybody saw the need; but nobody could see the man. Down

in Huntingdonshire a young farmer leans on the handles of his plough.

"The world needs a man, a good man, a great man, a strong man!" says his Reason. And then he hears another voice.

"Thou art the man!" cries his Conscience, with terrifying suddenness; and his hands tremble as they grasp the plough.

That evening, as he sits beside the fire, his young wife opposite him, and little Robert in the cot by his side, he takes down his Bible and reads. He turns to the Epistle to the Philippians, at the closing chapter. He is amazed at the things that, by the grace divine, Paul claims to have learned and achieved.

"It's true, Paul," he exclaims, "that *you* have learned this and attained to this measure of grace; but what shall I do? Ah, poor creature, it is a hard, hard lesson for me to take out! I find it so!"

Poring over the sacred volume, however, he makes the discovery of his lifetime. "I came," he says, "to the thirteenth verse, where Paul saith, *'I can do all things through Christ which strengtheneth me.'* Then faith began to work, and my heart to find comfort and support; and I said to myself, 'He that was *Paul's* Christ is *my* Christ too!' And so I drew water out of the Wells of Salvation!"

And now we have reached the fountain-head at last!

VI

And so the clodhopper became the king! It was *the text* that did it! Considered apart from the text, the life of Cromwell is an insoluble mystery, a baffling enigma. But take one good look at the text: observe the place that it occupied in Cromwell's heart and thought: and everything becomes plain. "That such a man, with the eye to see and with the heart to dare, should advance, from post to post, from victory to victory, till the Huntingdonshire Farmer became, by whatever name you call him, the acknowledged Strongest Man in England, virtually the King of England, requires," says Carlyle, "no magic to explain it." Of course not! The text explains it. For see!

What is a king? In his *French Revolution*, Carlyle says that the very word "king" comes from Kon-ning, Can-ning, The Man Who Can, the Man Who is Able! And that is precisely the burden of the text.

"I can do all things through Christ which strengtheneth me"; so the Authorized Version has it.

"In Him who strengthens me I am able for anything"; so Dr. Moffatt translates the words.

"For all things I am strong in Him who makes me able"; thus Bishop Moule renders it.

A King, says Carlyle, is an Able Man, a Strong Man, a Man who Can. Here is a ploughman who sees that the world is perishing for want of just such a King. How can he, weak as he is, become the world's Strong Man, the world's Able Man, the world's King? The text tells him.

VII

A man — at any rate such a man as Cromwell — can never be content to enjoy such an experience as this alone. No man can read the Life or Letters of the Protector without being touched by his solicitude for others. He is for ever anxious that his kindred and friends should drink of those wondrous waters that have so abundantly refreshed him and invigorated him. After quoting his text to Colonel Walton, he urges him to seek that same strengthening grace which he himself has received.

"Seek that!" he says; *"seek that!"*

It is the keynote of all his correspondence. "I hope," he writes to the Mayor of Hursley in 1650, "I hope you give my son good counsel; I believe he needs it. He is in the dangerous time of his age, and it is a very vain world. O how good it is to close with Christ betimes! There is nothing else worth looking after!"

"Seek that strength!" he says to Colonel Walton.

"Seek that Savior!" he says to his wayward son.

"Seek that which will really satisfy!" he says to his daughter.

It always seems to me that the old Puritan's lovely letter to that daughter of his, the letter from which I have just quoted, is the gem of Carlyle's great volume. Bridget was twenty-two at the time. "Your sister," her father tells her, "is exercised with some perplexed thoughts. She seeks her own vanity and carnal mind, and bewailing it, she seeks after what will satisfy. And thus to be a seeker is to be of the best sect next to a finder, and such an one shall every faithful humble seeker be at the end. Happy seeker; happy finder! Dear heart, press on! Let not husband, let not anything cool thy affections after Christ!"

With which strong, tender, fatherly words from the old soldier to his young daughter we may very well take leave of him.

6

BLAISE PASCAL
(1623-1662)

Blaise Pascal was a French religious philosopher, a mathematician, physicist, and mystic. An accident in 1654, in which he almost lost his life, brought him to a genuine conversion experience. His doctrine centered on the person of Christ and that one can experience God only through the heart rather than reason.

Pascal's work *Pensées,* a treatise on spirituality, has been translated into many languages. In English it is simply known as *Thoughts.* He also wrote a series of nineteen letters published under the title *Provincial Letters of Pascal,* in which he comes out as a champion of freedom of conscience, of truth, and of justice against the powerful Jesuits of his day.

His text: "For my people have committed two evils; they have forsaken me the fountain of living waters, and hewed them out cisterns, broken cisterns, that can hold no water" (Jeremiah 2:13).

I

The conversion of Blaise Pascal is one of the shining events in the stately history of the Christian church. Seldom has so mighty an intellect submitted with such perfect grace to the authority of the Savior. Pascal is not only one of the world's epoch-makers; he is one of the architects of civilization. Every day of our lives we all of us do things that, but for Pascal, we could never have done. Every day of our lives we enjoy comforts and privileges that, but for him, could never have been ours. His commanding personality and triumphant reason dominate human life at every turn. He is one of history's quiet conquerors; he does not advertise himself; his work does not lend itself to parade or display; yet, put him among the giants of the past, and most of them are instantly dwarfed by his presence. Few names, as Principal Tulloch says, are more classical than his. "Though cut off at the early age of thirty-nine, there is hardly any name more famous at once in literature, science, and religion." For three centuries every thinker of note has been profoundly influenced by him. The annals of France glitter with a multitude of brilliant personalities; but none of them shine with a lustre that is comparable to that of Pascal.

II

He was only a youth when he shook the dust of the world from his feet and entered upon the life of a lay solitary at Port Royal; yet the amazing thing is that, by that time, he had established a reputation for mathematical audacity, philosophical originality, and scientific ingenuity which no record in the world's long history can rival. He was, Bussuet says, endowed by Nature with all the gifts of understanding; a geometer of the first rank; a profound logician, a lofty and eloquent writer. If, Bossuet maintains, we scan a list of his inventions and discoveries, and then reflect that, in addition, he wrote one of the most perfect works that has ever appeared in the French language, and that in all his books there are passages of unrivalled eloquence and depth of reflection, we shall come to the conclusion that a greater genius never existed in any country or in any age. Again and again, while Pascal was a mere boy, Paris was electrified by his dazzling discoveries. As one reads the romantic and almost incredible story of those early years, it is impossible to repress a conjecture as to the part that he would have played in the history of the world, and the sensational changes that he would have effected, *if* he had persisted in the career to which he devoted his earlier years, and *if* he had been spared to old age in the pursuit of those researches.

The bent of his mind betrayed itself as soon as he was out of his cradle. Like John Stuart Mill, he was educated by his father. Like the elder Mill, the elder Pascal had ideas of his own concerning the intellectual development and ultimate career of his boy. But there is an essential difference between the two cases. John Stuart Mill loyally adopted his father's ideas and dutifully followed the path that had been prepared for his feet. Blaise Pascal, on the contrary, rebelled against the program mapped out for him, and eventually brought his father to his own way of thinking.

The elder Pascal was obsessed by one all-mastering prejudice. He was determined, come what might, that his boy should have nothing to do with mathematics. He was himself a mathematician, and experience had taught him that the study of mathematics captivates and monopolizes the mind to the exclusion of all other themes. He therefore set himself to guard his son's mind from all contact with mathematical lore. Every book that touched on mathematical problems was carefully concealed; in the presence of the boy the father rigidly abstained from discussing mathematical topics with his friends; and, to make matters absolutely secure, the father set his son such difficult lessons in Latin and other languages as would leave him neither time nor energy nor inclination for the speculations that he so ardently desired him to eschew. But, in all this, the elder Pascal resembles nothing so much as an anxious hen frantically endeavoring to teach her brood of ducklings to avoid the water towards which all the instincts of their nature are impelling them.

III

As a child Pascal was characterized by an extraordinary and insatiable curiosity. It was not merely the passive curiosity that smiles, wonders, and passes on: it was the active curiosity that insists on investigating the *why* and the *wherefore* of each arresting circumstance and phenomenon. He was little more than an infant when he noticed that a plate, struck with a knife, emits a loud and lingering sound; but that, as soon as a hand is laid upon it, the sound instantly ceases. Every child has noticed this, and has been interested and amused by it: but the matter has ended there. Pascal, however, immediately initiated a series of experiments based upon this curious happening. *Why* did the knife awaken the sound? *Why* did the fingers silence it? The boy was soon working out a philosophy of sounds. His father had forbidden his meddling with geometry in any form; but the temptation was too great. In the secrecy of his own room he kept a supply of charcoal and a few boards. On these he practiced making circles that should be perfectly round, triangles whose angles should be exactly equal, and other figures of the kind. Working away by himself, he came, quite independently, to many of the conclusions elaborated by Euclid. On one such occasion, the father crept into the room on tiptoe. The boy was so engrossed in his demonstrations that for some time he was unaware of his father's presence. The father stood for a while dumbfounded. He felt as the hen may be supposed to feel when she sees the ducklings well out on the pond. He recognized that the boy was in his element. Startled by the brilliance of his son's genius, he left the room without saying a word. And, with a wisdom that does him credit, he strode off to the city to secure for the youth teachers who would be able to assist him along the line for which he had so obvious a bent.

At the age of sixteen Pascal wrote his famous treatise of Conic Sections. The most brilliant Frenchmen of the time were staggered. With one accord they declared that it was the most powerful and valuable contribution that had been made to mathematical science since the days of Archimdedes. While still in his teens, Pascal made up his mind that Science, to fulfil its destiny, must relate itself to the industry and commerce of the workaday world. Acting on this principle, he began by inventing a calculating machine and finished by inventing, on his deathbed, the commonplace but useful vehicle that we now call an omnibus. The difficulties involved in the construction of the calculating machine prevented its being of much use to his own generation; but, later on, those obstacles were overcome, and the contrivance of Pascal paved the way for all the cash registers and adding-machines of our modern shops and offices. But perhaps the greatest triumph of Pascal's genius was his discovery that atmosphere has definite weight, and that the level of the mercury varies in different altitudes and in different weather. Sir David Brewster has given us a vivid and amusing description of the experiments made by Pascal first at the base, and then at the summit, of the Puy-de-Dome on the memorable day on which he established his historic conclusions. On that day — Saturday, September 19, 1648 — Pascal virtually gave us the barometer, and thus made a contribution to the science of meteorology which it is impossible now to overvalue. This triumph led him to his prolonged series of researches concerning the equilibrium of fluids; and there are those who regard his treatise on this subject as his crowning achievement. But, however that may be, there he stands! He is still in the twenties; yet all the world knows him as a thinker of unsurpassed brilliance and audacity; as a scientist who knows how to harness the most profound erudition to the most practical ends; and as a writer who can express the most obtruse [*sic*] ideas in language that a little child can understand.

IV

The greatest day in Pascal's life was the day of his conversion. Except in the light of that momentous happening, his biography is unintelligible. As Dean Church puts it, the religion of Pascal is essentially the religion of a converted man. He was thirty-one at the time; and so overwhelming was the flood-tide of divine grace that came surging into his heart that, to the day of his death, he wore stitched into his doublet a piece of parchment on which he had recorded the exact hour of that unforgettable experience. It was *in the year of grace 1654, on Monday the twenty-third of November, from half-past ten in the evening until half an hour after midnight.*

Yet while in *one* sense, that conversion of his was so sudden and cataclysmic that he can chronicle with the utmost definiteness the precise moment at which it took place, there is *another* sense in which it was very gradual. I can trace its slow development. Eight years earlier, in 1646, a number of excellent books had fallen into his hands. This course of reading so affected him, his sister tells us, that he came to the conclusion that, to be a Christian, a man ought to live only for God and to seek no object but His pleasure. "This became so evident to my brother, and so imperative, that he relinquished for a time all his scientific researches and set himself to seek that *one thing needful* of which our Lord has spoken."

Having once applied himself to this sublime quest, he kept his eyes wide open. The most arresting object on his horizon was the exquisite beauty of his sister's life. In earlier days, *his* studious ways had rebuked her frivolity and led her to seriousness: now *her* devotion shames his worldliness. She led a life of such sweetness, unselfishness, and charm that her very presence was a perpetual benediction on everybody in the house. It was a poignant grief to her to see her brother, to whom she felt that she owed the grace that she herself enjoyed, bemoaning the destitution of his own soul. She saw him frequently, pitied him increasingly, and pleaded with him to abandon everything that clogged his spirit and to yield himself without reserve to the Savior.

The momentous crisis was precipitated at length by accident.

"One day," says Bossuet, "when he went to take his daily drive to the bridge of Neuilly in a carriage and four, the two leading horses became restive at a point at which the road was bounded by a parapet over the river. They reared and plunged and eventually to the horror of the onlookers, flung themselves over the stonework into the Seine. Fortunately, the first strokes of their feet broke the traces which bound them to the pole, and the carriage hung suspended on the brink of the parapet. The effect of such a shock on a man of Pascal's feeble health may be imagined. He swooned away, and was only restored with difficulty. His nerves were so shattered that, long afterwards, during sleepless nights and moments of weakness, he seemed to see a precipice at his bedside over which he was on the point of falling." This happened in October, 1654; a month later he found joy and peace in believing. "On the night of the twenty-third of November," says Madame Duclaux, "he found himself unable to sleep, and lay in bed reading the Scriptures. Suddenly his eyes dazzled; a flame of fire seemed to envelop him. Such a moment of marvellous euphoria could never be forgotten, and, in mortal words, could never be expressed. It found natural utterance in floods of tears and in that fragmentary speech which, like so many sobs, Pascal employs in that mystic Memorial which thenceforth he ever wore in secret, sewn into his clothes like a talisman." Here it is:

FIRE!

Certainty! Joy! Peace!
I forget the world and everything but God!
Righteous Father, the world hath
not known Thee, but I have known Thee!
Joy, Joy, Joy! Tears of Joy!
Jesus!
Jesus!
I separated myself from Him; renounced and
crucified Him!
They have forsaken ME, the fountain of living
waters!
I separated myself from HIM!
May I not be separated from Him eternally!
I submit myself absolutely to
JESUS CHRIST MY REDEEMER.

In that hour, Blaise Pascal, the mightiest thinker of his time, was converted! "All in a moment," as Viscount St. Cyres puts it, "he was touched by God. He was caught in the grip of a mysterious Power. Some strange spiritual chemistry blotted out his former tastes and inclinations and left him a new being." He himself called it his conversion; and, in order that others might share with him the rapture of so radiant an experience, he sat down almost at once and wrote his treatise *On the Conversion of the Sinner*. And, if ever we are tempted to suppose that his fire-baptism was simply one moment of frenzy punctuating a life of scholarly frigidity, we are confronted by the significant circumstance that, to his dying day, he wore the Memorial next his heart. He was loyal to his vision to the end. "And so," he wrote, when nearing his goal, "and so I stretch forth my hands to my Redeemer, who came to earth to suffer and to die for me." In that faith — so simple yet so sublime — so personal yet so profound — Pascal rested serenely to the last.

V

"My people have committed two evils: they have forsaken Me, the fountain of living waters, and hewed out to themselves cisterns, broken cisterns, that can hold no water." This is the passage that was running in Pascal's mind that November midnight; and he inscribed it across the very center of his historic Memorial.

"His eyes had been opened," says Dean Church. "He felt himself touched and overcome by the greatness and the reasonableness of things unseen. He consciously turned to God, not from vice, but from the bondage of the interests of time, from the fascination of a merely intellectual life and from the frivolity which forgets the other world in this."

Here then are "the cisterns, the broken cisterns, that can hold no water" — "the bondage of the interests of time; from the fascination of a merely intellectual life; the frivolity which forgets the other world in this!"

And here is *the fountain of living waters* that he for so long forsook! Jesus! Jesus! Jesus! Jesus Christ my Redeemer! From that November midnight, Jesus was everything to Pascal — *everything!* "His whole argument," says Viscount St. Cyres, "centers in the person of the Redeemer." "To him," says Principal Tulloch, "Christ was the only solution of all human perplexities." From the age of thirty-one to the day of his death, at the age of thirty-nine, he had but one desire: he lived that he might turn the thoughts of men to his Savior.

It may be that, during those last years of his brief life, he devoted less time to science, although, as his biographers are careful to show, he by no means relinquished it. But, as against this, we must remember that, during those closing years, he wrote a book that will be treasured as long as the world stands. Lord Avebury included it in his list of the best books ever written. And nobody has read Pascal's *Thoughts* without being lifted by it into a clearer atmosphere, and helped to a loftier plane.

Blaise Pascal was endowed with a soul of singularly delicate texture. He had a mind that was amazingly sensitive to all those vibrations by which truth reveals itself to men; he had an eye that was quick to see beauty in whatever form it presented itself; he had a heart that insistently hungered for the sublime. In his early days he saw the *High* and it entranced him; but on that never-to-be-forgotten November night, he saw the *Highest*. Without reserve and without delay he laid all his marvellous faculties of heart and brain at the feet of the Savior who, that night, had revealed Himself in such a bewildering wealth of power and grace.

7

JOHN BUNYAN

(1628-1688)

John Bunyan was an English Puritan preacher, best known for writing *Pilgrim's Progress*. This well-known allegory has been translated into more than a hundred languages and dialects, and has been read by more people than any other book except the Bible.

Bunyan married a praying Christian lady who led him to Jesus Christ. Shortly after his conversion, he joined the Bedford Baptist Church and began to preach. In 1660 he was imprisoned for preaching without permission from the established church. He remained in prison for over twelve years.

During his imprisonment Bunyan wrote his autobiography, *Grace Abounding*, and *Pilgrim's Progress*. He also wrote *Life and Death of Mr. Badman* and a second allegory, *The Holy War*.

John Bunyan died in London and was buried in Bunhill Field, a traditional burying ground for the nonconformists of his day.

His text: "Him that cometh to me I will in no wise cast out" (John 6:37).

I

There is no doubt about John Bunyan's text. As a lover carves his lady's name on trees, signs it in mistake for his own, and mutters it in his sleep, so Bunyan inscribes everywhere the text that wrought his memorable deliverance. It crops up again and again in all his writings. The characters in his allegories, the dream-children of his fertile fancy, repeat it to each other as though it were a password, a talisman, a charm; he himself quotes it whenever the shadow of an opportunity presents itself; if it is not the text, it is at least the burden, of every sermon that he preaches. It sings itself through his autobiography like a repeating chorus, like an echoing refrain. By its radiance he extricates himself from every gloomy valley and from every darksome path. Its joyous companionship beguiles all his long and solitary tramps. It dispels for him the loneliness of his dreary cell. When no other visitor is permitted to approach the jail, John Bunyan's text comes rushing to his memory as though on angel's wings. It sings to him its song of confidence and peace every morning; its music scatters the gloom of every night. It is the friend of his fireside; the companion of his solitude; the comrade of his travels; the light of his darkness. It illumines his path mid the perplexities of life; it wipes away his tears in the day of bitter sorrow; and it smooths his pillow in the hour of death.

When a man habitually wears a diamond pin, you unconsciously associate the thought of his face with the thought of the gem that scintillates beneath it. In the same way, nobody can have become in the slightest degree familiar with John Bunyan without habitually associating the thought of his honest and rugged personality with the thought of the text that he made so peculiarly his own.

II

On the opening pages of *Pilgrim's Progress* we come upon the principal character, all clothed in rags, a heavy burden upon his back, greatly distressed in mind, walking in the fields and crying, "What must I do to be saved?"

"Do you see yonder shining light?" asks Evangelist.

"I think I do," replied the wretched man.

"Keep that light in your eye and go directly thereto; so shalt thou see a gate, at which, when thou knockest, it shall be told thee what thou shalt do!"

The man comes in due course to the gate and knocks many times, saying:

> May I now enter here? Will he within
> Open to sorry me, though I have been
> An undeserving rebel? Then shall I
> Not fail to sing his lasting praise on high.

"I am willing with all my heart," replies Good Will, the keeper of the gate, "we make no objection against any. Notwithstanding all that they have done before they come hither, they are *in no wise cast out!*"

So Christian enters in at the gate and sets out on pilgrimage. And there, at the very beginning of his new life, stands the first vague but unmistakable suggestion of John Bunyan's text.

"In no wise cast out!"

"In no wise cast out!"

"Him that cometh to Me, I will in no wise cast out!"

There, over the portal of the pilgrim path, stands the text that gave John Bunyan to the world.

III

It stands over the very portal of his pilgrim's path for the simple reason that it stands at the very beginning of his own religious experience. Let us turn from his allegory to his autobiography.

"In no wise cast out!" he exclaims. "Oh, the comfort that I found in that word!"

"In no wise cast out!"

"In no wise cast out!"

We all know the story of the wretchedness which that great word dispelled. It is one of the most moving records, one of the most pathetic plaints, in the language. Bunyan felt that he was a blot upon the face of the universe. He envied the toads in the grass by the side of the road, and the crows that cawed in the ploughed lands by which he passed. They, he thought, could never know such misery as that which bowed *him* down. "I walked," he says, in a passage that Macaulay felt to be specially eloquent and notable, "I walked to a neighboring town, and sat down upon a settle in the street, and fell into a very deep pause about the most fearful state my sin had brought me to; and, after long musing, I lifted up my head; but methought I saw as if the sun that shineth in the heavens did grudge to give me light; and as if the very stones in the street, and tiles upon the houses, did band themselves against me. Methought that they all combined together to banish me out of the world. I was abhorred of them, and unfit to dwell among them, because I had sinned against the Savior. Oh, how happy now was every creature over me, for they stood fast and kept their station. But I was gone and lost!"

"Gone and lost!"
"Gone and lost!"

It was while he was thus lamenting his hopeless condition that the light broke. "This scripture," he says, "did most sweetly visit my soul: *'and him that cometh to Me, I will in no wise cast out.'* O, the comfort that I had from this word!"

"In no wise cast out!"
"In no wise cast out!"
"Him that cometh to Me, I will in no wise cast out!"

What was it that he saw in "that blessed sixth of John"? What was the comfort that he found so lavishly stored there? The matter is worth investigating.

IV

In his pitiful distress, there broke upon the soul of John Bunyan a vision of the infinite *approachability* of Jesus. That is one of the essentials of the faith. It was for no other purpose that the Savior of men left the earth and enshrined Himself in invisibility. "Suppose," says Henry Drummond, "suppose He had not gone away; suppose He were here now. Suppose He were still in the Holy Land, at Jerusalem. Every ship that started for the East would be crowded with Christian pilgrims. Every train flying through Europe would be thronged with people going to see Jesus. Every mail-bag would be full of letters from those in difficulty and trial. Suppose you are in one of those ships. The port, when you arrive after the long voyage, is blocked with vessels of every flag. With much difficulty you land, and join one of the long trains starting for Jerusalem. Far as the eye can reach, the caravans move over the desert in an endless stream. As you approach the Holy City you see a dark, seething mass stretching for leagues and leagues between you and its glittering spires. You have come to see Jesus; but you will never see Him."

You are crowded out. Jesus resolved that this should never be. "It is expedient for you," He said, "that I go away." He went away in order to make Himself approachable! John Bunyan saw to his delight that it is possible for the most unworthy to go direct to the fountain of grace.

"Him that *cometh to Me!*"
"Him that *cometh to Me!*"
"Him that *cometh to Me,* I will in no wise cast out!"

John Bunyan's text was a revelation to him of the *approachability* of Jesus.

V

In his pitiful distress there broke upon the soul of John Bunyan a vision of the infinite *catholicity* of Jesus. Therein lay for him the beauty of the text. In the darkest hours of his wretchedness he never had any doubt as to the readiness of the Savior to welcome to His grace certain fortunate persons. Holy Master Gifford, for example, and the poor women whom he overheard discussing the things of the kingdom of God as they sat in the sun beside their doors, and the members of the little church at Bedford; concerning the salvation of these people Bunyan was as clear as clear could be.

But from such felicity he was himself rigidly excluded. "About this time," he says, "the state of happiness of these poor people at Bedford was thus, in a kind of a vision, presented to me. I saw as if they were on the sunny side of some high mountain, there refreshing themselves with the pleasant beams of the sun, while I was shivering and shrinking in the cold, afflicted with frost, snow, and dark clouds. Methought also, betwixt me and them, I saw a wall that did compass about this mountain. Now through this wall my soul did greatly desire to pass; concluding that, if I could, I would there also comfort myself with the heat of their sun." But he could find no way through or round or over the wall. Then came the discovery of the text. "This scripture did most sweetly visit my soul; *'and him that cometh to Me, I will in no wise cast out.'* Oh! the comfort that I had from this word, *in no wise!* As who should say, *'By no means,* for nothing whatever he hath done.' But Satan would greatly labor to pull this promise from me, telling me that Christ did not mean me and such as me, but sinners of another rank, that had not done as I had done. But I would answer him again. 'Satan, there is in these words no such exception; but him that cometh, him, any him; *him that cometh to Me I will in no wise cast out.'* "

"*Him that cometh!*"

"*Any him! Any him!*"

"*Him that cometh I will in no wise cast out!*"

Like the gate that swings open on hearing the magic "sesame"; like the walls that fell at Jericho when the blast of the trumpets arose; the wall round Bunyan's mountain fell with a crash before that great and golden word. *"Him that cometh to Me I will in no wise cast out!"* The barriers had vanished! The way was open!

"Him that cometh!"

"Any him! Any him!"

"Him that cometh to Me I will in no wise cast out!" Here was a vision of the *catholicity* of Jesus!

VI

In his pitiful distress there broke upon the soul of John Bunyan a vision of the infinite *reliability* of Jesus. It was the deep, strong accent of certainty that ultimately captivated all his heart. Times without number, he had come with a great "perhaps" trembling on his lips. "Often," he tells us, "when I had been making to the promise, I have seen as if the Lord would refuse my soul for ever, I was often as if I had run upon the pikes, and as if the Lord had thrust at me to keep me from Him, as with a flaming sword. Then would I think of Esther, who went to petition the king contrary to the law. I thought also of Benhadad's servants, who went with ropes under their heads to their enemies for mercy. The woman of Canaan, that would not be daunted, though called 'dog' by Christ; and the man that went to borrow bread at midnight, were also great encouragements to me." But each was, after all, only the encouragement of possibility, of a probability, of a "perhaps."

Perhaps! Perhaps! Perhaps!

In contrast with all this, the text spoke out its message bravely. *"Him that cometh to Me I will in no wise cast out!"*

"In no wise! In no wise! In no wise!"

"Oh! the comfort that I had from this word: *'in no wise!'* . . . If ever Satan and I did strive for any word of God in all my life, it was for this good word of Christ: he at one end and I at the other. Oh! what work we made! It was for this in John, I say, that we did so tug and strive; he pulled, and I pulled; but God be praised, I overcame him; I got sweetness from it!"

He passed at a bound from the Mists of the Valley to the Sunlight of the Summit. He had left the shadowland of "perhaps" for the luxurious sunshine of a glowing certainty. "With joy," he says, "I told my wife: 'Oh, now *I know, I know, I know!'* That was a good night to me; I have had but few better. Christ was a precious Christ to my soul that night; I could scarce lie in my bed for joy and grace and triumph!"

Perhaps! Perhaps! Perhaps!
In no wise! In no wise! In no wise!
I know! I know! I know!
Thus Bunyan found in the radiance that streamed from "that blessed sixth of John," a revelation of the *reliability* of Jesus!

VII

Those who have studied Butler's *Analogy of Religion* will recall the story that, in the introductory pages, Mr. Malleson tells of the illustrious author. When Bishop Butler lay upon his deathbed, Mr. Malleson says, an overwhelming sense of his own sinfulness filled him with a terrible concern. His chaplain bent over him and tried to comfort him.

"You know, sir," said the chaplain, "that Jesus is a great Savior!"

"Yes," replied the terror-stricken bishop, "I know that He died to save. But how shall I know that He died to save *me?*"

"My lord," answered the chaplain, "it is written that *him that cometh to Me I will in no wise cast out!*"

"True!" exclaimed the dying man, "I am surprised that, though I have read that scripture a thousand times over, I never felt its virtue until this moment. Now I die happy!"

And he did.

So, too, pillowing his head upon the selfsame words, did Bunyan. "His end," says Froude, "was characteristic. It was brought on by exposure when he was engaged in an act of charity. A quarrel had broken out in a family at Reading with which Bunyan had some acquaintance. A father had taken some offence at his son, and threatened to disinherit him. Bunyan undertook a journey on horseback from Bedford to Reading in the hope of reconciling them. He succeeded, but at the cost of his life. Returning by way of London, he was overtaken on the road by a storm of rain, and was drenched before he could find shelter. The chill, falling on a constitution already weakened by illness, brought on fever. In ten days he was dead. His last words were: 'Take me, for I come to Thee!'"

"I come to Thee! I come to Thee!"
"Him that cometh to Me, I will in no wise cast out!"
The words that had lit up the path of his pilgrimage illumined also the valley of the shadow of death! The words that opened to him the realms of grace opened also the gates of glory! The words that had welcomed him at the Wicket Gate welcomed him also to the Celestial City!

8

JOHN WESLEY

(1703-1791)

John Wesley was the founder of Methodism. The Church of
England closed its doors to Wesley because of his enthusiasm.
He preached to various literature societies and, at the persuasion
of George Whitefield, preached to the unchurched masses in the
open air. In his itineraries he often rode fifteen to twenty miles
on horseback, preaching four to five times a day. At times there
were 10,000 to 30,000 people waiting to hear him preach. It is
said that he traveled 250,000 miles in the British Isles, preaching
between 40,000 and 50,000 sermons.

The American Methodists were formed in 1784 and by 1850
had become the largest Protestant church in America. At the
time of his death, Wesley had more than 120,000 followers in
England.

His text: "Christ Jesus came into the world to save sinners; of
whom I am chief" (1 Timothy 1:15).

I

John Wesley made history wholesale. "You cannot cut him out
of our national life," Mr. Augustine Birrell declares. If you could,
the gap would be as painful as though you had overthrown the
Nelson column in Trafalgar Square or gashed Mount Everest out
of the Himalaya Ranges. Lecky, who is a pastmaster in the art of
analyzing great movements and in tracing the psychological
influences from which they sprang, says that the conversion of
John Wesley formed one of the grand epochs of English history.

His conversion, mark you! Lecky goes on to say that the religious revolution begun in England by the preaching of the Wesleys is of greater historic importance than all the splendid victories by land and sea won under Pitt. The momentous event to which the historian points, be it noted, is not Wesley's birth, but his re-birth. It is his conversion that counts.

In order that I may scrutinize once more the record of that tremendous event in our national annals, I turn afresh to Wesley's journal. It was on May 24, 1738. Wesley was engaged in those days in a persistent and passionate quest. He had crossed the Atlantic as a missionary only to discover the waywardness and wickedness of his own evil heart. "What have I learned?" he asks himself when he finds himself once more on English soil. "What have I learned? Why, I have learned what I least of all suspected, that I, who went to America to convert the Indians, was never myself converted to God!"

One day, early in 1738, he is chatting with three of his friends when all at once they begin to speak of their faith, the faith that leads to pardon, the faith that links a man with God, the faith that brings joy and peace through believing. Wesley feels that he would give the last drop of his blood to secure for himself such an unspeakable treasure. Could such a faith be his? he asks his companions. "They replied with one mouth that this faith was the gift, the free gift of God, and that He would surely bestow it upon every soul who earnestly and perseveringly sought it." Wesley made up his mind that, this being so, it should be his. "I resolved to seek it unto the end," he says. "I continued to seek it," he writes again, "until May 24, 1738." And, on May 24, 1738, he found it! That Wednesday morning, before he went out, he opened his Bible haphazard, and a text leapt out at him. *"Thou art not very far from the kingdom of God!"* It strangely reassured him.

"The kingdom of God!"
"Far from the kingdom of God!"
"Not very far from the kingdom of God!"

How far? He was so near that, that very evening, he entered it! *"In the evening,"* he says, in the entry that has become one of the monuments of English literature, *"in the evening I went very unwillingly to a society in Aldersgate Street, where one was reading Luther's preface to the Epistle to the Romans. About a quarter before nine, while he was describing the change which God works in the heart through faith in Christ, I felt my heart strangely warmed. I felt that I did trust in Christ, Christ alone, for salvation: and an assurance was given me that He had taken away my sins, even mine, and saved me from the law of sin and death."*

Here is a sailor! He finds himself far, far from port, with no chart, no compass, no hope of ever reaching his desired haven! Later on, he shades his eyes with his hand and actually sees the bluff headlands that mark the entrance to the harbor: he is not very far from the city of his desire! And, later still, the bar crossed and the channel found, he finds himself lying at anchor in the bay.

So it was with John Wesley. When he returned from Georgia, he was far, very far from the kingdom of God. When he opened his Bible that Wednesday morning, he was not very far from the kingdom of God. And that same evening, at Aldersgate Street, he passed through the gates into the light and liberty of the kingdom.

So far from the kingdom!
Not far from the kingdom!
The kingdom! The kingdom! The kingdom of God!

II

It is a beautiful thing to have been brought near to the kingdom of God. Many influences combined to bring John Wesley near. To begin with, he had a mother; one of the most amazing mothers that even England — that land of noble mothers — has produced. Susanna Wesley was a marvel of nature and a miracle of grace. To begin with, she was the twenty-fifth child of her father; and, to go on with, she had nineteen children of her own! And she found time for each of them. In one of her letters, she tells how deeply impressed she was on reading the story of the evangelistic efforts of the Danish missionaries in India. "It came into my mind," she says, "that I might do more than I do. I resolved to begin with my own children. I take such proportion of time as I can best spare to discourse every night with each child by itself." Later on, people began to marvel at her remarkable influence over her children. "There is no mystery about the matter," she writes again, "I just took Molly alone with me into my own room every Monday night, Hetty every Tuesday night, Nancy every Wednesday, Jacky every Thursday, and so on; that was all!" Yes, that was all; but see how it turned out! "I cannot remember," says John Wesley, "I cannot remember ever having kept back a doubt from my mother; she was the one heart to whom I went in absolute confidence, from my babyhood until the day of her death." Such an influence could only tend to bring him *near to the kingdom of God.*

Then there was the fire! John never forgot that terrible night. He was only six. He woke up to find the old rectory ablaze from the ground to the roof. By some extraordinary oversight, he had been forgotten when everybody else was dragged from the burning building. In the nick of time, just before the roof fell in with a crash, a neighbor, by climbing on another man's shoulders, contrived to rescue the terrified child at the window. To the last day of his life Wesley preserved a crude picture of the scene. And underneath it was written, "Is not this a brand plucked from the burning?" It affected him as a somewhat similar escape affected Clive. "Surely God intends to do some great thing by me that He has so miraculously preserved me!" exclaimed the man who afterwards added India to the British empire. When a young fellow of eighteen, Richard Baxter was thrown by a restive horse under the wheel of a heavy wagon. Quite unaccountably, the horses instantly stopped. "My life was miraculously saved," he wrote, "and I then and there resolved that it should be spent in the service of others." Dr. Guthrie regarded as one of the potent spiritual influences of his life his marvellous deliverance from being dashed to pieces over a precipice at Arbroath. In his *Grace Abounding*, Bunyan tells how he was affected by the circumstance that the man who took his place at the siege of Leicester was shot through the head while on sentry duty and killed instantly. Such experiences tend to bring men within sight of the kingdom of God. Wesley never forgot the fire.

III

It is a great thing to recognize that, though near to the kingdom, one is still outside.

Sir James Simpson, the discoverer of chloroform, used to say that the greatest discovery that he ever made was the discovery that he was a sinner and that Jesus Christ was just the Savior he needed. John Wesley could have said the same. But, whereas Sir James Simpson was able to point to the exact date on which the sense of his need broke upon him, John Wesley is not so explicit. He tells us that it was in Georgia that he discovered that he, the would-be converter of Indians, was himself unconverted. And yet, before he left England, he wrote to a friend that his chief motive in going abroad was the salvation of his own soul. As soon as he arrived on the other side of the Atlantic, he made the acquaintance of August Spangenberg, a Moravian pastor. A conversation took place which Wesley records in his journal as having deeply impressed him.

"My brother," said the devout and simple-minded man whose counsel he had sought, "I must ask you one or two questions. Do you know Jesus Christ?"

"I know," replied Wesley, after an awkward pause, "I know that he is the Savior of the world."

"True," answered the Moravian, "but do you know that He has saved *you?*"

"I hope He has died to save me," Wesley responded.

The Moravian was evidently dissatisfied with these vague replies, but he asked one more question.

"Do you know yourself?"

"I said that I did," Wesley tells us in his journal, "but I fear they were vain words!"

He saw others happy, fearless in the presence of death, rejoicing in a faith that seemed to transfigure their lives. What was it that was *theirs* and yet not *his?* "Are they read in philosophy?" he asks. "So was I. In ancient or modern tongues? So was I also. Are they versed in the science of divinity? I, too, have studied it many years. Can they talk fluently upon spiritual things? I could do the same. Are they plenteous in alms? Behold, I give all my goods to feed the poor! I have labored more abundantly than they all. Are they willing to suffer for their brethren? I have thrown up my friends, reputation, ease, country; I have put my life in my hand, wandering into strange lands; I have given my body to be devoured by the deep, parched up with heat, consumed by toil and weariness. But does all this make me acceptable to God! Does all this make me a Christian? By no means! I have sinned and come short of the glory of God. I am alienated from the life of God. I am a child of wrath. I have no hope." It is a great thing, I say, for a man who has been brought within sight of the kingdom to recognize frankly that he is, nevertheless, still outside it.

IV

It is a fine thing for a man who feels that he is outside the kingdom to enter into it.

In his *Cheapside to Arcady,* Mr. Arthur Scammell describes the pathetic figure of an old man he often saw in a London slum. "He had crept forth from some poor house hard by, and, propped up by a crutch, was sitting on the edge of a low wall in the unclean, sunless alley, while, only a few yards further on, was the pleasant open park, with sunshine, trees, and flowers, the river and fresh air, and, withal, a more comfortable seat: but the poor old man never even looked that way. I have often seen him since, always in the same place, and felt that I should like to ask him why he sits there in darkness, breathing foul air, when the blessed sunshine is waiting for him only ten yards off."

So near to the sunshine!

So near to the kingdom!

Unlike Mr. Scammell's old man, John Wesley made the great transition from shadow to sunshine, from squalor to song.

"Dost thou believe," asks Staupitz, the wise old monk, "dost thou believe in the forgiveness of sins?"

"I believe," replied Luther, reciting a clause from his familiar credo, "I believe in the forgiveness of sins!"

"Ah," exclaimed the elder monk, "but you must not only believe in the forgiveness of David's sins and Peter's sins, for this even the devils believe. It is God's command that we believe *our own sins* are forgiven us!"

"From that moment," says D'Aubigné, "light sprung up in the heart of the young monk at Erfurt."

"I believed," says Luther, "that *my sins, even mine,* were forgiven me!"

"I did trust in Christ, Christ alone, for salvation," says Wesley, in his historic record, "and an assurance was given me that He had taken away *my sins, even mine!"*

The analogy is suggested by the circumstance that it was Luther's commentary that was being read aloud at Aldersgate Street that night.

"My sins, even mine!" says Luther.

"My sins, even mine!" says Wesley.

Forty-five years afterwards Mr. Wesley was taken very ill at Bristol and expected to die. Calling Mr. Bradford to his bedside, he observed: "I have been reflecting on my past life. I have been wandering up and down, these many years, endeavouring, in my poor way, to do a little good to my fellow creatures; and now it is probable that there is but a step between me and death; and what have I to trust to for salvation? I can see nothing which I

have done or suffered that will bear looking at. I have no other
plea than this:

> *I the chief of sinners am,*
> *But Jesus died for me."*

Eight years later — fifty-three years after the great change at
Aldersgate Street — he was actually dying. As his friends surrounded his bedside, he told them that he had no more to say. "I
said at Bristol," he murmured, "that

> I the chief of sinners am,
> But Jesus died for me."

"Is that," one asked, "the present language of your heart, and
do you feel now as you did then?"

"I do," replied the dying veteran.

This, then, was the burden of Wesley's tremendous ministry
for more than fifty-three years. It was the confidence of his life
and the comfort of his death. It was his first thought every morning and his last every night. It was the song of his soul, the breath
of his nostrils, and the light of his eyes. This was the gospel that
transfigured his own experience; and this was the gospel by
which he changed the face of England. "John Wesley," says Mr.
Birrell, "paid more turnpikes than any man who ever bestrode a
beast. Eight thousand miles was his annual record for many a
long year, during each of which he seldom preached less frequently than a thousand times. No man ever lived nearer the
center than John Wesley, neither Clive, nor Pitt, nor Johnson. No
single figure influenced so many minds; no single voice touched
so many hearts. No other man did such a life's work for England." "The eighteenth century," says President Wilson, "cried
out for deliverance and light; and God prepared John Wesley to
show the world the might and the blessing of His salvation."

V

The pity of it is that John Wesley was thirty-five when he
entered the kingdom. The zest and vigor of his early manhood
had passed. He was late in finding mercy. Thirty-five! Before
they reached that age, men like Murray McCheyne, Henry Martyn,
and David Brainerd had finished their life-work and fallen into
honored graves.

Why was Wesley's great day so long in coming? He always felt that the fault was not altogether his own. He groped in the dark for many years and nobody helped him — not even his ministers. William Law was one of those ministers, and Wesley afterwards wrote him on the subject. "How will you answer to our common Lord," he asks, "that you, sir, never led me into the light? Why did I scarcely ever hear you *name the name of Christ?* Why did you never urge me to *faith in His blood?* Is not Christ the First and the Last? If you say that you thought I had faith already, verily, you know nothing of me. I beseech you, sir, by the mercies of God, to consider whether the true reason of your never pressing this salvation upon me was not this — *that you never had it yourself!*"

Here is a letter for a man like Wesley to write to a man like Law! Many a minister has since read that letter on his knees and has prayed that he may never deserve to receive so terrible a reprimand.

9

GEORGE WHITEFIELD
(1714-1770)

George Whitefield was an English evangelist, perhaps best known for his open-air preaching both in Great Britain and America.

It was at Oxford that Whitefield met Charles Wesley and later John Wesley. This was the beginning of a long friendship, even though they were to go their separate ways due to doctrinal differences.

Whitefield made seven visits to America, where he founded an orphanage in Savannah, Georgia. He died and was buried in Newburyport, Massachusetts. It is said that in thirty-four years of ministry, he preached more than 18,000 sermons.

His text: "Verily, verily, I say unto thee, Except a man be born again, he cannot see the kingdom of God" (John 3:3).

I

George Whitefield was the first man who treated Great Britain and America as if they both belonged to him. He passed from the one to the other as though they were a pair of rural villages, and he was the minister in charge of the parish. George Whitefield took a couple of continents under his wing; and the wing proved capacious enough for the task.

In days when the trip was a serious undertaking, he crossed the Atlantic thirteen times; but, of all his voyages, this was the worst. Day after day, ploughing her way through terrific seas, the good ship has shuddered in the grip of the gale. The sailors were at their wits' end: the sails were torn to ribbons and the tackling was all strained and broken. George Whitefield, who, wrapped in a buffalo hide, sleeps in the most protected part of the vessel, has been drenched through and through twice in one night. The ship has been so buffeted and beaten that nearly three months have passed before the Irish coast is sighted. Rations have been reduced to famine fare. The gravest anxiety marks every countenance.

Today, however, there is a lull in the storm. The seas have moderated and the sun is shining. In the afternoon, Mr. Whitefield assembles the passengers and crew, and conducts a service on the deck. Have a good look at him!

He is twenty-five, tall, graceful, and well-proportioned; of fair complexion and bright blue eyes. There is a singular cast in one of those eyes, which, though not unsightly, has the curious effect of making each hearer feel that the preacher is looking directly at him. There is something extraordinarily commanding about him; it was said that, by raising his hand, he could reduce an unruly rabble of twenty thousand people to instant silence.

His voice, strong and rich and musical, was so perfectly modulated and controlled that his audiences were charmed into rapt attention. It had phenomenal carrying power. While Whitefield was preaching in the open-air one day, Benjamin Franklin, who was present, made a singular computation. He walked backwards until he reached a point at which he could no longer hear every word distinctly. He marked the spot and afterwards measured the distance. As a result, he calculated that Mr. Whitefield could command an audience of thirty thousand people without straining his voice in the least.

Today, however, instead of thirty thousand people, he has barely thirty. Standing on the hatchway, with a coil of rope at his feet, he announces his text: *"Verily, verily, I say unto thee, Except a man be born again, he cannot see the kingdom of God."* The passengers lounging about the deck, and the sailors leaning against the bulwarks, listen breathlessly as, for half an hour, an earnest and eloquent man pours out his heart in personal testimony, powerful exposition, and passionate entreaty. "Every man," he cries, "who has even the least concern for the salvation of his precious and immortal soul should never cease watching and praying and striving till he find a real, inward, saving change wrought in his heart, and thereby doth know of a truth that he has been *born again.*"

"Verily, verily, I say unto thee, Except a man be born again, he cannot see the kingdom of God." That is George Whitefield's text in mid-Atlantic because it is George Whitefield's text on both sides of the Atlantic. In season and out of season, in public and in private, he ceaselessly proclaimed that message. He felt that he was sent into the world to call the attention of men to that one mandatory word. He is known to have preached more than three hundred times from this memorable and striking passage. And nobody who has read the story of his spiritual travail will marvel for a moment at his having done so.

II

For it was that great text about *the new birth* that had thrown open to him the gates of the kingdom of God. He was only a schoolboy when it first dawned upon him that, between him and that kingdom, a frightful chasm yawned. "I got acquainted," he says, "with such a set of debauched, abandoned, atheistical youths that if God, by His free grace, had not delivered me out of their hands, I should long ago have sat in the scorner's chair. I took pleasure in their lewd conversation. My thoughts of religion became more and more like theirs. I affected to look rakish, and was in a fair way of being as infamous as the worst of them." Then came the sudden arrest, the quick realization of his folly; and the vision of the hideous blackness of his own heart. But how to cure it? That was the problem. He resolved to change, at any rate, his *outward* bearing. "As, once, I affected to look more rakish, so now I strove to appear more grave than I really was." This, however, was cold comfort; it was like painting rotten wood: he was conscious all the time of the concealed corruption. He tried another course. He denied himself every luxury; wore ragged and even dirty clothes; ate no foods but those that were repugnant to him; fasted altogether twice a week; gave his money to the poor; and spent whole nights in prayer lying prostrate on the cold stones or the wet grass. But it was all of no avail. He felt that there was something radically wrong in the very heart of him, something that all this penance and self-degradation could not change. Then came the Angel of Deliverance; and the Angel of Deliverance bore three golden keys. One was a *man;* one was a *book;* one was a *text.*

The *man* was Charles Wesley, the minstrel of Methodism. George Whitefield and Charles Wesley were, by this time, fellow-students at Oxford. Wesley noticed the tall, grave youth, always walking alone, apparently in deep thought; and he felt strangely drawn to him. They met. Forty years afterwards Charles Wesley commemorated that meeting:

> Can I the memorable day forget,
> When first we by divine appointment met?
> Where undisturbed the thoughtful student roves,
> In search of truth, through academic groves;
> A modest pensive youth, who mused alone,
> Industrious the beaten path to shun,
> An Israelite, without disguise or art,
> I saw, I loved, and clasped him to my heart,
> A stranger as my bosom friend caressed,
> And unawares received an angel-guest!

But, if Whitefield was "an angel-guest" to Charles Wesley, Charles Wesley was certainly no less to Whitefield. Whitefield often referred to him as "my never-to-beforgotten friend." In those days Charles Wesley also was groping after the light: he could not, therefore, solve his new friend's aching problem, but he could lend him the books that he himself was reading; and he did.

The *book* that Charles Wesley lent George Whitefield was Henry Scougal's *The Life of God in the Soul of Man*. He read it with amazement and delight. It told him exactly what he longed to know. He learned for the first time that true religion is a union of the soul with God: it is Christ formed within us. "When I read this," he says, "a ray of divine light instantaneously darted in upon my soul; and, from that moment, but not till then, did I know that I must become *a new creature.*" He is a young man of twenty-one. "After having undergone innumerable buffetings by day and night, God was pleased at length," he says, "to remove my heavy load and to enable me, by a living faith, to lay hold on His dear Son. And oh! with what joy — joy unspeakable and full of glory — was I filled when the weight of sin left me and an abiding sense of the pardoning love of God broke in upon my disconsolate soul!" His first act in his ecstasy was to write to all his relatives. "I have found," he tells them, "that there is such a thing as *the new birth.*"

"I must be a new creature!"

"There is such a thing as the new birth!"

"Verily, verily, I say unto thee, Except a man be born again, he cannot see the kingdom of God!"

It was thus that the *man* introduced the *book;* and the *book* introduced the *text;* and the *text* led George Whitefield into the kingdom of God. "I know the exact place," he says. "It may perhaps be superstitious, but, whenever I go to Oxford, I cannot help running to the spot where Jesus Christ first revealed Himself to me and gave me *a new birth.*"

III

A new creature!
The new birth!
"Except a man be born again . . ."
What does it mean? It means, if it means anything, that the miracle of Creation's morning may be re-enacted: a man may be made all over again. He may be changed root and branch: the very fibre and fabric of his manhood may be transfigured. You ask me to explain this *new* creation: I will do so when you have explained the *earlier* one. You ask me to explain this *second* birth: I merely remind you that the *first* birth — the physical and intellectual one — is involved in inscrutable mystery.

I cannot explain the creation of the universe; but, for all that, here is *the universe!*

I cannot explain the mystery of birth; but what does it matter? here is *the child!*

I cannot explain the truth that, darting like a flash of lightning into the soul of that Oxford student, transforms his whole life; but, explained or unexplained, here is *George Whitefield!*

"O Lord," muttered Alexander Pope one day, "make me a *better* man!"

"It would be easier," replied his spiritually-enlightened page, "to make you a *new* man!"

And in that distinction lies the whole doctrine that so startled and captivated and dominated the life of George Whitefield.

IV

With this text burned into his very soul, and inscribed indelibly upon his mind, George Whitefield mapped out the program of his life. He set himself to a stupendous and world-wide campaign; he determined that he would carry that one message everywhere. He was forever on the march; and he was forever and ever proclaiming, with the most affecting fervour and persuasion, that *except a man be born again, he cannot see the kingdom of God.*

David Garrick used to say that he would gladly give a hundred guineas to be able to pronounce the word "Oh!" as movingly as Whitefield did. The secret was that all Whitefield's soul was in that yearning monosyllable. He was hungry for the salvation of men. He remembered his own bewilderment, his own frantic struggle for freedom; and he longed to shed upon others the light that had broken so startlingly and joyously upon him. He could scarcely speak of anything else. In preaching a funeral sermon soon after Mr. Whitefield's death, the Rev. Joseph Smith said that "there was scarcely one sermon in which Mr. Whitefield did not insist upon the necessity of *the new birth*. With passionate vehemency and earnest repetition he cried again and again: *Verily, verily, I say unto thee, Except a man be born again, he cannot see the kingdom of God.*" He found that the hearts of men were waiting wistfully for that message.

He tells us, for example, of one of his earliest efforts. It was at Kingswood. He was refused permission to preach in the church unless he would undertake to say nothing about *the new birth*. But that was the very subject on which he was determined to speak. He therefore resorted to the open fields; and the miners, in their thousands, thronged around him. "I preached," he says, "on the Savior's word to Nicodemus, *Ye must be born again;* and the people heard me gladly. Having no righteousness of their own to renounce, they were delighted to hear of One who came not to call the righteous but sinners to repentance. The first discovery of their being affected was to see the white gutters made by the tears which streamed plentifully down their black cheeks as they came fresh from the coalpit. Hundreds and hundreds of them were soon brought under deep convictions which happily ended in sound and thorough conversion. The change was visible to all."

The news spread through the country that a cultured and eloquent preacher was declaring to great multitudes on village greens, at street corners, at fairs and fetes, at festivals, on bowling greens and in open fields that men might be remade, regenerated, *born again*. The inhabitants of towns that he had not yet visited sent to him, begging him to come. When, for example, he was approaching Bristol, multitudes went out on foot to meet him; and the people saluted and blessed him as he passed along the street. The churches were so crowded that it was with difficulty that he could obtain access to the pulpit. Some hung upon the rails of the organ loft; others climbed upon the leads of the church; at every crack and crevice ears were straining to catch the message. When he preached his last sermon in the town, and told the people that they would see his face no more, they all — high and low, young and old — burst into tears. Multitudes followed him to his rooms weeping; the next day he was employed from daylight till midnight in counselling eager inquirers; and, in the end, he left the town secretly at dead of night, in order to evade the throng that would have insisted on attending him.

V

George Whitefield made the doctrine of *the new birth* his universal message because he found that it met a universal need. I catch glimpses of him under many skies and under strangely varied conditions; but he is always proclaiming the same truth, and always with the same result.

Here he is, seated with an Indian in a canoe on one of the great American rivers! He is visiting the various encampments of the Delawares. He loves to go from tribe to tribe, and from wigwam to wigwam, telling the red men, by the aid of an interpreter, that a man of any kind and any color may be *born again*. For hundreds of miles, he trudges his way through the solitudes of the great American forests that he may deliver to Indians and backwoodsmen the message that is burning in his soul.

Here he is, preaching to the black men of Bermuda! *"Except,"* he cries, *"except a man be born again, he cannot see the kingdom of God."* "Attention," he tells us, "sat on every face. I believe there were few dry eyes. Even the negroes who could not get into the building, and who listened from without, wept plentifully. Surely a great work is begun here!"

Here he is in Scotland! He is visiting Cambuslang; and there is no building large enough to accommodate any considerable fraction of the crowds that throng to hear him. He therefore preaches in the glen. The grassy level by the burnside, and the steep brae which rises from it in the form of an amphitheatre, offer a noble and impressive auditorium. "He dwelt mostly on *Regeneration,"* the record tells us. And the result vindicated his choice of a theme. On the last Sunday of his stay he preached to between thirty and forty thousand people, while over three thousand participated in the closing communion.

Here he is in the Countess of Huntingdon's drawing-room! The sumptuous apartment is thronged by princes and peers, philosophers and poets, wits and statesmen. To this select and aristocratic assembly he twice or three times every week delivers his message. *"Ye must be born again!"* he says; and he implores his titled hearers to seek the regenerating grace that can alone bring the joy of heaven into the experiences of earth.

Here he is, bending over his desk. He is writing to Benjamin Franklin — "the man who wrenched the scepter from tyrants and the lightning from heaven." "I find," he says, "that you grow more and more famous in the learned world. As you have made such progress in investigating the mysteries of electricity, I now humbly urge you to give diligent heed to the mystery of *the new birth*. It is a most important and interesting study, and, when mastered, will richly repay you for your pains."

I could change the scene indefinitely. But in every country, and under every condition, he is always expatiating on one tremendous theme:

"Verily, verily, I say unto thee, Except a man be born again, he cannot see the kingdom of God."

He cannot help it. When, at Oxford, he first discovered the necessity, and experienced the power, of *the new birth*, he could speak of nothing else. "Whenever a fellow-student entered my room," he says, "I discussed with him our Lord's words about being *born again.*" For thirty years he preached night and day on the theme that had torn the shackles from his own soul. Towards the close of his *Life of George Whitefield*, Mr. J. P. Gledstone gives a list of the eminent preachers, poets, and philanthropists who, together with thousands of less famous men, were led into the kingdom and service of Christ as a result of Mr. Whitefield's extraordinary ministry. He often said that he should like to die in the pulpit, or immediately after leaving it; and he almost had his wish. He preached the day before he died; and he remained true to his own distinctive message to the last. "I am now fifty-five years of age," he said, in one of these final addresses, "and I tell you that I am more than ever convinced that the truth of *the new birth* is a revelation from God Himself, and that without it you can never be saved by Jesus Christ."

"Why, Mr. Whitefield," inquired a friend one day, "why do you so often preach on *Ye must be born again?*"

"Because," replied Mr. Whitefield, solemnly, looking full into the face of his questioner, "because *ye must be born again!*"

That is conclusive. It leaves nothing more to be said!

10

JOHN NEWTON
(1725-1807)

John Newton, a seaman, slave trader, and for a time a slave himself, sank to the lowest depths of sin — living a life of "continual godlessness and profanity." He later said, "I never met a man with a more vile mouth than mine. I wasn't even content with the common oaths everyone knew. I invented new ones everyday — some so vivid that the captain, a blasphemer himself, would bawl me out."

Over and over again Newton's life had been spared — by missing an appointment or by a change of plans not of his doing. While on a ship bound for England from the banks of Newfoundland, a violent storm hit, and in desperation he found himself asking God for mercy. The ship was spared. He was no longer an infidel, and he was freed from the habit of swearing. But it was not until sometime later that his life was transformed and he became a powerhouse for God.

His text: "And thou shalt remember that thou wast a bondman . . . and the Lord thy God redeemed thee" (Deuteronomy 15:15).

I

John Newton was plagued with a terribly treacherous memory. In his youth it had betrayed and nearly ruined him; how could he ever trust it again? "You must know," said Greatheart to Christiana's boys, "you must know that Forgetful Green is the most dangerous place in all these parts." John Newton understood, better than any man who ever lived, exactly what Greatheart meant. Poor John Newton nearly lost his soul on Forgetful Green. His autobiography is filled with the sad, sad story of his forgettings. "I forgot," he says again and again and again, "I forgot . . . ! I soon forgot . . . ! This, too, I totally forgot!" The words occur repeatedly. And so it came to pass that when, after many wild and dissolute years, he left the sea and entered the Christian ministry, he printed a certain text in bold letters, and fastened it right across the wall over his study mantelpiece:

> THOU SHALT REMEMBER THAT THOU WAST
> A BONDMAN IN THE LAND OF EGYPT, AND THE
> LORD THY GOD REDEEMED THEE.

A photograph of that mantelpiece lies before me as I write. There, clearly enough, hangs John Newton's text! In sight of it he prepared every sermon.

In this respect John Newton resembled Thomas Goodwin. "When," says that sturdy Puritan, in a letter to his son, "when I was threatening to become cold in my ministry, and when I felt Sabbath morning coming and my heart not filled with amazement at the grace of God, or when I was making ready to dispense the Lord's Supper, do you know what I used to do? I used to take a turn up and down among the sins of my past life, and I always came down again with a broken and contrite heart, ready to preach, as it was preached in the beginning, the forgiveness of sins." "I do not think," he says again, "I ever went up the pulpit stair that I did not stop for a moment at the foot of it and take a turn up and down among the sins of my past years. I do not think that I ever planned a sermon that I did not take a turn round my study-table and look back at the sins of my youth and of all my life down to the present; and many a Sabbath morning, when my soul had been cold and dry for the lack of prayer during the week, a turn up and down in my past life before I went into the pulpit always broke my hard heart and made me close with the gospel for my own soul before I began to preach." Like this great predecessor of his, Newton felt that, in his pulpit preparation, he must keep his black, black past ever vividly before his eyes.

"I forgot . . . ! I soon forgot . . . ! This, too, I totally forgot!"

"Thou shalt remember, remember, remember!"

"Thou shalt remember that thou wast a bondman in the land of Egypt, and that the Lord thy God redeemed thee!"

II

"A bondman!"
"Thou shalt remember that thou wast a bondman!"
The words were literally true! For some time Newton was a
slave trader; but, worse still, for some time he was a slave! Newton's conversion deserves to be treasured among the priceless
archives of the Christian Church because of the amazing transformation it effected. It seems incredible that an Englishman
could fall as low as he did. As Professor Goldwin Smith says, he
was a brand plucked from the very heart of the burning! Losing
his mother — the one clear guiding-star of his early life — when
he was seven, he went to sea when he was eleven. "I went to
Africa," he tells us, "that I might be free to sin to my heart's
content." During the next few years his soul was seared by the
most revolting and barbarous of all human experiences. He
endured the extreme barbarities of a life before the mast; he fell
into the pitiless clutches of the pressgang; as a deserter from the
navy he was flogged until the blood streamed down his back; and
he became involved in the unspeakable atrocities of the African
slave trade.

And then, going from bad to worse, he actually became a slave
himself! The slave of a slave! He was sold to a negress who,
glorying in her power over him, made him depend for his food on
the crusts that she tossed under her table! He could sound no
lower depth of abject degradation. In the after-years, he could
never recall this phase of his experience without a shudder. As he
says in the epitaph that he composed for himself, he was "the
slave of slaves."
"A bondman!"
"A slave of slaves! A bondman of bondmen!"
"Thou shalt remember that thou wast a bondman!"
How could he ever forget?

III

How, I say, could he ever forget? And yet he had forgotten
other things scarcely less notable.

As a boy, he was thrown from a horse and nearly killed. Looking death in the face in this abrupt and untimely way, a deep
impression was made. "But," he says, *"I soon forgot!"*
Some years later, he made an appointment with some compan-

ions to visit a man-of-war. They were to meet at the waterside at a certain time and row out to the battleship. But the unexpected happened. Newton was detained; his companions left without him; the boat was upset, and they were drowned. "I went to the funeral," Newton says, "and was exceedingly affected. *But this, also, I soon forgot!*"

Then came a remarkable dream. Really, he was lying in his hammock in the forecastle of a ship homeward bound from Italy. But, in his fancy, he was back at Venice. It was midnight; the ship, he thought, was riding at anchor; and it was his watch on deck. As, beneath a clear Italian sky, he paced to and fro across the silent vessel, a stranger suddenly approached him. This mysterious visitant gave him a beautiful ring. "As long as you keep it," he said, "you will be happy and successful; but, if you lose it, you will know nothing but trouble and misery." The stranger vanished. Shortly after, a second stranger appeared on deck. The newcomer pointed to the ring. "Throw it away!" he cried, "throw it away!" Newton was horrified at the proposal; but he listened to the arguments of the stranger and at length consented. Going to the side of the ship, he flung the ring into the sea. Instantly the land seemed ablaze with a range of volcanoes in fierce eruption, and he understood that all those terrible flames had been lit for his destruction. The second stranger vanished; and, shortly after, the first returned. Newton fell at his feet and confessed everything. The stranger entered the water and regained the ring. "Give it me!" Newton cried, in passionate entreaty, "give it me!" "No," replied the stranger, "you have shown that you are unable to keep it! I will preserve it for you, and, whenever you need it, will produce it on your behalf." "This dream," says Newton, "made a very great impression; but the impression soon wore off, and, in a little time, *I totally forgot it!*"

"I forgot!"

"This, too I soon forgot!"

"In a little time, I totally forgot it!"

So treacherous a thing was Newton's memory! Is it any wonder that he suspected it, distrusted it, feared it? Is it any wonder that, right across his study wall, he wrote that text?

"Thou shalt remember!"

"Thou shalt remember that thou wast a bondman!"

"Thou shalt remember that thou wast a bondman, and that the Lord thy God redeemed thee!"

IV

"Thou shalt remember that thou wast a bondman!"
"Thou shalt remember that the Lord thy God redeemed thee!"
But how? Was the work of grace in John Newton's soul a sudden or a gradual one? It is difficult to say. The birth of the body is a very sudden and yet a very gradual affair: so also is the birth of the soul. To say that John Newton was *suddenly* converted would be to ignore those gentle and gracious influences by which two good women — his mother and his sweetheart — led him steadily heavenwards.

"I was born," Newton himself tells us, "in a home of godliness, and dedicated to God in my infancy. I was my mother's only child, and almost her whole employment was the care of my education." Every day of her life she prayed with him as well as for him, and every day she sought to store his mind with those majestic and gracious words that, once memorized, can never be altogether shaken from the mind. It was the grief of her deathbed that she was leaving her boy, a little fellow of seven, at the mercy of a rough world; but she had sown the seed faithfully, and she hoped for a golden harvest.

Some years later, John Newton fell in love with Mary Catlett. She was only thirteen — the age of Shakespeare's Juliet. But his passion was no passing fancy. "His affection for her," says Professor Goldwin Smith, "was as constant as it was romantic; his father frowned on the engagement, and he became estranged from home; but through all his wanderings and sufferings he never ceased to think of her; and after seven years she became his wife." The Bishop of Durham, in a centennial sermon, declares that Newton's pure and passionate devotion to this simple and sensible young girl was "the one merciful anchor that saved him from final self-abandonment." Say that Newton's conversion was sudden, therefore, and you do a grave injustice to the memory of two women whose fragrant influence should never be forgotten.

And yet it *was* sudden; so sudden that Newton could tell the exact date and name the exact place! It took place on the tenth of March, 1748, on board a ship that was threatening to founder in the grip of a storm. *"That tenth of March,"* says Newton, *"is a day much to be remembered by me; and I have never suffered it to pass unnoticed since the year 1748. For on that day — March 10, 1748 — the Lord came from on high and delivered me out of deep waters.* " The storm was terrific: when the ship went plunging down into the trough of the seas few on board expected her to come up again. The hold was rapidly filling with water. As Newton hurried to his place at the pumps he said to the captain, "If this will not do, the Lord have mercy upon us!" His own words startled him.

"Mercy!" he said to himself, in astonishment, "mercy! *mercy!* What mercy can there be for me? This was the first desire I had breathed for mercy for many years! About six in the evening the hold was free from water, and then came a gleam of hope. I thought I saw the hand of God displayed in our favor. I began to pray. I could not utter the prayer of faith. I could not draw near to a reconciled God and call Him Father. My prayer for mercy was like the cry of the ravens, which yet the Lord Jesus does not disdain to hear."

"In the gospel," says Newton, in concluding the story of his conversion, "in the gospel I saw at least a peradventure of hope; but on every other side I was surrounded with black, unfathomable despair." On that "peradventure of hope" Newton staked everything. On the tenth of March, 1748, he sought mercy — and found it! He was then twenty-three.

V

Years afterwards, when he entered the Christian ministry, John Newton began making history. He made it well. His hand is on the nation still. He changed the face of England. He began with the church. In his *History of the Church of England,* Wakeman gives us a sordid and terrible picture of the church as Newton found it. The church was in the grip of the political bishop, the fox-hunting parson, and an utterly worldly and materialistic laity. Spiritual leadership was unknown. John Newton and a few kindred spirits, "the first generation of the clergy called 'Evangelical,' " became — to use Sir James Stephen's famous phrase — "the second founders of the Church of England." There is scarcely a land beneath the sun that has been unaffected by Newton's influence. As one of the founders of the Church Missionary Society, he laid his hand upon all our continents and islands.

Through the personalities of his converts, too, he wielded a power that it is impossible to compute. Take two, by way of illustration. Newton was the means of the conversion of Claudius

Buchanan and Thomas Scott. In due time Buchanan carried the gospel to the East Indies, and wrote a book which led Adoniram Judson to undertake his historic mission to Burma. Scott became one of the most powerful writers of his time, and, indeed, of all time. Has not Cardinal Newman confessed that it was Scott's treatment of the doctrine of the Trinity that preserved his faith, in one of the crises of his soul, from total shipwreck?

And what ought to be said of Newton's influence on men like Wilberforce and Cowper, Thornton and Venn? One of our greatest literary critics has affirmed that the friendship of Newton saved the intellect of Cowper. "If," said Prebendary H. E. Fox, not long ago, "if Cowper had never met Newton, the beautiful hymns in the Olney collection, and that notable poem, 'The Task' — nearest to Milton in English verse — would never have been written."

Moreover, there are Newton's own hymns. Wherever, to this day, congregations join in singing "How Sweet the Name of Jesus Sounds," or "Glorious Things of Thee Are Spoken," or "One There Is Above All Others," or "Amazing Grace, How Sweet the Sound," *there* John Newton is still at his old task, still making history!

VI

And, all the time, the text hung over the fireplace:
"Thou shalt remember!"
"Thou shalt remember that thou wast a bondman!"
"Thou shalt remember that the Lord thy God redeemed thee!"
From that time forth Newton's treacherous memory troubled him no more. He never again forgot. He never could. He said that when, from the hold of the sinking ship, he cried for mercy, it seemed to him that the Savior looked into his very soul.

> Sure, never till my latest breath,
> Can I forget that look;
> It seemed to charge me with His death,
> Though not a word He spoke.

"I forgot . . . ! I soon forgot . . . ! This, too, I totally forgot!"
"Thou shalt remember that the Lord thy God redeemed thee!"
"Never till my latest breath can I forget that look!"
The Rev. Richard Cecil, M.A., who afterwards became his

biographer, noticing that Newton was beginning to show signs of age, urged him one day to stop preaching and take life easily. "What!" he replied, "shall the old African blasphemer stop while he can speak at all?" He could not forget. And he was determined that nobody else should! In order that future generations might know that he was a bondman and had been redeemed, he wrote his own epitaph and expressly directed that this — this and no other — should be erected for him:

> JOHN NEWTON,
> Clerk,
> Once an Infidel and Libertine,
> A Servant of Slaves in Africa,
> was
> by the Mercy of our Lord and Savior
> Jesus Christ,
> Preserved, Restored, Pardoned,
> And Appointed to Preach the Faith he
> had so long labored to destroy.

No; that treacherous memory of his never betrayed him again! When he was an old, old man, very near the close of his pilgrimage, William Jay, of Bath, one day met him in the street. Newton complained that his powers were failing fast. "My memory," he said, "is nearly gone; but I remember two things, that I am a great sinner and that Christ is a great Savior!"

"Thou shalt remember that thou wast a bondman in the land of Egypt, and that the Lord thy God redeemed thee!" — that was John Newton's text.

"My memory is nearly gone; but I remember two things, that I am a great sinner, and that Christ is a great Savior!" — that was John Newton's testimony.

"I forgot...! I soon forgot...! This, too, I totally forgot!"

"Thou shalt remember, remember, remember!"

Newton liked to think that the memory that had so basely betrayed him — the memory that, in later years, he had so sternly and perfectly disciplined — would serve him still more delightfully in the life beyond. Cowper died a few years before his friend; and Newton liked to picture to himself their reunion in heaven. He wrote a poem in which he represented himself as grasping Cowper's hand and rapturously addressing him:

Oh! let thy memory wake! I told thee so;
I told thee thus would end thy heaviest woe;
I told thee that thy God would bring thee here,
And God's own hand would wipe away thy tear,
While I should claim a mansion by thy side;
I told thee so - for our Emmanuel died.

"Oh! let thy memory wake!"
"I forgot. . .! I soon forgot. . .! This, too, I totally forgot!"
"Thou shalt remember that the Lord thy God redeemed thee!"
Newton felt certain that the joyous recollection of that infinite
redemption would be the loftiest bliss of the life that is to be.

11

WILLIAM CAREY
(1761-1834)

William Carey is often called "the father of modern missions."
He was a man of determination, and although born into the
home of a poor weaver and schoolteacher, he learned Latin,
Greek, Hebrew, French, and Dutch while in his teens and could
read the Bible in six languages. This interest in languages
became a great asset to him in India where as a missionary he
established the Serampore Printing Press. The Bible or portions
of it were published in thirty-six languages or dialects through
his efforts.

In addition to preaching and translating the Scriptures, Carey
and his co-workers translated Indian classics into English and
produced grammars and dictionaries in various Indian languages.

The Serampore Press made the Bible available to more than
three hundred million people.

His text: "Lengthen thy cords, and strengthen thy stakes; for
thou shalt break forth on the right hand and on the left; and thy
seed shall inherit the Gentiles, and make the desolate cities to be
inhabited" (Isaiah 54:2-3).

I

The westering sun, slanting through the tops of the taller trees,
is beginning to throw long shadows across the green and gently
undulating fields. The brindled cattle, lying at their ease and
meditatively chewing the cud in these quiet Northamptonshire
pastures, are disturbed by the sound of footsteps in the lane.

Some of them rise in protest and stare fixedly at the quaint figure that has broken so rudely on their afternoon reverie. But he causes them no alarm, for they have often seen him pass this way before. He is the village cobbler. This very morning he tramped along this winding thoroughfare on his way to North-ampton. He was carrying his wallet of shoes — a fortnight's work — to the Government contractor there. And now he is trudging his way back to Moulton with the roll of leather that will keep him busy for another week or two. The cattle stare at him, as well they may. The whole world would stare at him if it had the chance today. For this is William Carey, the harbinger of a new order, the prophet of a new age, the maker of a new world!

The cattle stare at him, but he has no eyes for them. His thoughts are over the seas and far away. He is a dreamer; but he is a dreamer who means business. Less than twenty years ago, in a tall chestnut tree not far from this very lane, he spied a bird's nest that he greatly coveted. He climbed — and fell! He climbed again — and fell again! He climbed a third time, and, in the third fall, broke his leg. A few weeks later, while the limb was still bandaged, his mother left him for an hour or two, instructing him to take the greatest care of himself in her absence. When she returned, he was sitting in his chair, flushed and excited, *with the bird's nest on his knees.*

"Hurrah, mother; I've done it at last! Here it is, look!"

"You don't mean to tell me you've climbed that tree again!"

"I couldn't help it, mother; I couldn't, really! *If I begin a thing I must go through with it!*"

On monuments erected in honor of William Carey, on bu' and plaques and pedestals, on the title pages of his innumerai biographies, and under pictures that have been painted of hir, I have often seen inscribed some stirring sentence that fell from his eloquent lips. But I have never seen that one. Yet the most characteristic word that Carey ever uttered was the reply that he made to his mother that day!

"If I begin a thing I must go through with it!"

If you look closely, you will see that sentence stamped upon his countenance as, with a far-away look in his eye, he passes down the lane. Let us follow him, and we shall find that he is beginning some tremendous things; and, depend upon it, he will at any cost go through with them!

II

It is not an elaborately furnished abode, this little home of his. For, although he is a minister, schoolmaster, and cobbler, the three vocations only provide him with about thirty-six pounds a year. Looking around, I can see but a few stools, his cobbler's outfit, a book or two (including a Bible, a copy of Captain Cook's Voyages, and a Dutch Grammar) besides a queer-looking map on the wall. We must have a good look at this map, for there is history in it as well as geography. It is a map of the world, made of leather and brown paper, and it is the work of his own fingers.

Look, I say, at this map, for it is a reflection of the soul of Carey. As he came up the lane, looking neither to the right hand nor to the left, he was thinking of the world. He is a jack-of-all-trades, yet he is a man of a single thought. "Perhaps," he says to himself, "perhaps God means what He says!" The world! The World! *The World!* God so loved *the world!* Go ye into all *the world!* The kingdoms of *the world* shall become the kingdoms of our God and of His Christ! It is always the world, the world, *the world.*

That thought haunted the mind of Carey night and day. The map of the world hung in his room, but it only hung in his room because it already hung in his heart. He thought of it, he dreamed of it, he preached of it. And he was amazed that, when he unburdened his soul to his brother-ministers, or preached on that burning theme to his little congregation, they listened with respectful interest and close attention, yet *did nothing.*

At length, on May 31, 1792, Carey preached his great sermon, the sermon that gave rise to our modern missionary movement, the sermon that made history. It was at Nottingham. *"Lengthen thy cords"* — so ran the text — *"lengthen thy cords and strengthen thy stakes, for thou shalt break forth on the right hand and on the left; and thy seed shall inherit the Gentiles and make the desolate cities to be inhabited."*

"Lengthen thy cords!" said the text.

"Strengthen thy stakes!" said the text.

"Expect great things from God!" said the preacher.

"Attempt great things for God!" said the preacher.

"If all the people had lifted up their voices and wept," says Dr. Ryland, "as the children of Israel did at Bochim, I should not have wondered at the effect; it would only have seemed proportionate to the cause; so clearly did Mr. Carey prove the criminality of our supineness in the cause of God!" But the people did not weep! They did not even wait! They rose to leave as usual. When Carey, stepping down from the pulpit, saw the people quietly dispersing, he seized Andrew Fuller's hand and wrung it in an agony of distress. "Are we not going to *do anything?*" he demanded. "Oh, Fuller, call them back, call them back! We dare not separate *without doing anything!*" As a result of that passionate entreaty, a missionary society was formed, and William Carey offered himself as the Society's first missionary.

"If I begin a thing I must go through with it!" he said, as a schoolboy.

"We dare not separate without doing something!" he cried, as a young minister.

"Lengthen the cords! Strengthen the stakes!"

"Expect great things! Attempt great things!"

III

I can never think of William Carey without thinking of Jane Conquest. In the little hamlet by the sea, poor Jane watched through the night beside the cot of her dying child. Then, suddenly, a light leapt in at the lattice, crimsoning every object in the room. It was a ship on fire, and no eyes but hers had seen it! Leaving her dying boy to the great Father's care, she trudged through the snow to the old church on the hill.

> She crept through the narrow window and climbed the belfry stair,
> And grasped the rope, sole cord of hope for the mariners in despair.
> And the wild wind helped her bravely, and she wrought with
> an earnest will,
> And the clamorous bell spake out right well to the hamlet under the hill.
> And it roused the slumbering fishers, nor its warning task gave o'er
> Till a hundred fleet and eager feet were hurrying to the shore;
> And the lifeboat midst the breakers, with a brave and gallant few,
> O'ercame each check and reached the wreck
> and saved the hapless crew.

Upon the sensitive soul of William Carey there broke the startling vision of a world in peril, and he could find no sleep for his eyes nor slumber for his eyelids until the whole church was up and doing for the salvation of the perishing millions. It has been finely said that when, towards the close of the eighteenth century, it pleased God to awaken from her slumbers a drowsy and lethargic church, there rang out, from the belfry of the ages, a clamorous and insistent alarm; and, in that arousing hour, the hand upon the bellrope was the hand of William Carey.

"We dare not separate without doing something!"
"Lengthen the cords! Strengthen the stakes!"
"Expect great things! Attempt great things!"
"Here am I; send me, send me!"

IV

Now the life of William Carey is both the outcome and the exemplification of a stupendous principle. That principle was never better stated than by the prophet from whose flaming lips Carey borrowed his text. *"Thine eyes,"* said Isaiah, *"Thine eyes shall see the king in His beauty: they shall behold the land that stretches very far off."* The vision *kingly* stands related to the vision *continental;* the revelation of the Lord leads to the revelation of the limitless landscape.

What was it that happened one memorable day upon the road to Damascus? It was simply this: Saul of Tarsus saw the King in His Beauty! And what happened as a natural and inevitable consequence? There came into his life the passion of the far horizon. All the narrowing limits of Jewish prejudice and the cramping bonds of Pharisaic superstition fell from him like the scales that seemed to drop from his eyes. The world is at his feet. Single-handed and alone, taking his life in his hands, he storms the great centers of civilization, the capitals of proud empires, in the name of Jesus Christ. No difficulty can daunt him; no danger impede his splendid progress. He passes from sea to sea, from island to island, from continent to continent.

The hunger of the earth is in his soul; there is no coast or colony to which he will not go. He feels himself a debtor to Greek and to barbarian, to bond and to free. He climbs mountains, fords rivers, crosses continents, bears stripes, endures imprisonments, suffers shipwreck, courts insult, and dares a thousand deaths out of the passion of his heart to carry the message of hope to every crevice and corner of the earth. A more thrilling story of hazard, hardship, heroism, and adventure has never been written.

On the road to Damascus Paul saw the King in His beauty, and he spent the remainder of his life in exploiting the limitless landscape that unrolled itself before him. The vision of the *king* opened to his eyes the vision of the *continents*.

In every age these two visions have always gone side by side. In the *fourteenth* century, the vision of the King broke upon the soul of John Wickliffe. Instantly, there arose the Lollards, scouring city, town, and hamlet with the new evangel, the representatives of the instinct of the far horizon. The *fifteenth* century contains two tremendous names. As soon as the world received the vision *kingly* by means of Savonarola, it received the vision *continental* by means of Christopher Columbus.

In the *sixteenth* century, the same principle holds. It is, on the one hand, the century of Martin Luther, and, on the other, the century of Raleigh, Drake, Hawkins, Frobisher, Grenville, and the great Elizabethan navigators. All the oceans of the world became a snowstorm of white sails. The *seventeenth* century gave us, first the Puritans, and then the sailing of the *Mayflower*.

So we come to the *eighteenth* century. And the *eighteenth* century is essentially the century of John Wesley and of William Carey. At Aldersgate Street the vision of the King in His beauty dawned graciously upon the soul of John Wesley. During the fifty years that followed, that vision fell, through Wesley's instrumentality, upon the entire English people. The Methodist revival of the eighteenth century is one of the most gladsome records in the history of Europe. And then, John Wesley having impressed upon all men the vision of the *King*, William Carey arose to impress upon them the vision of the *Continents*.

"We must do something!" he cried.

"Lengthen the cords! Strengthen the stakes!"

"Expect great things! Attempt great things!"

"The King! The King! The Continents! The Continents!"

V

Having gazed upon these things, our eyes are the better fitted to appreciate the significance of the contents of the cobbler's room. There he sits at his last, the Bible from which he drew his text spread out before him, and a home-made map of the world upon the wall! There is no element of chance about that artless record. There is a subtle and inevitable connection between the two. In the *Bible* he saw the King in His beauty: on the *map* he caught glimpses of the far horizon. To him the two were inseparable; and, moved by the Vision of the Lord which he caught in the one, and by the Vision of the limitless landscape which he caught in the other, he left his last and made history.

VI

"Lengthen the cords! Strengthen the stakes!"
"Expect great things! Attempt great things!"
"Do something! Do something!"

It was at Nottingham that Carey preached that arousing sermon: it was in India that he practiced it. With the eye of a statesman and of a strategist he saw that the best way of regaining the ground that was being lost in Europe was to achieve new conquests in Asia. History abounds in striking coincidences; but, among them all, there is none more suggestive than the fact that it was on November 11, 1793 — the very day on which the French revolutionists tore the Cross from Notre Dame, smashed it on the streets, and abjured Christianity — that William Carey sailed up the Hooghly, landed at Calcutta, and claimed a new continent for Christ! And, like a statesman and a strategist, he settled down to do in India the work to which he had challenged the church at home.

"Lengthen the cords!"
"Strengthen the stakes!"

He started an indigo factory; made himself the master of a dozen languages; became Professor of Bengali, Sanskrit, and Mahratta at a salary of fifteen hundred a year; all in order to engage more and still more missionaries and to multiply the activities by which the Kingdom of Christ might be set up in India. His work of translation was a marvel in itself.

"If I begin a thing I must go through with it!" he said that day with the bird's nest on his lap.

"Do something! Do something!" he said in his agony as he saw the people dispersing after his sermon.

And in India he did things. He toiled terribly. But he sent the gospel broadcast through the lengths and breadths of that vast land; built up the finest college in the Indian Empire; and gave the peoples the Word of God in their own tongue.

VII

Just before Carey died, Alexander Duff arrived in India. He was a young Highlander of four-and-twenty, tall and handsome, with flashing eye and quivering voice. Before setting out on his own life-work he went to see the man who had changed the face of the world. He reached the college on a sweltering day in July. "There he beheld a little yellow old man in a white jacket, who tottered up to the visitor, received his greetings, and with outstretched hands, solemnly blessed him." Each fell in love with the other. Carey, standing on the brink of the grave, rejoiced to see the handsome and cultured Scotsman dedicating his life to the evangelization and emancipation of India. Duff felt that the old man's benediction would cling to his work like a fragrance through all the great and epoch-making days ahead.

Not long after, Carey lay dying, and, to his great delight, Duff came to see him. The young Highlander told the veteran of his admiration and his love. In a whisper that was scarcely audible, the dying man begged his visitor to pray with him. After he had complied, and taken a sad farewell of the frail old man, he turned to go. On reaching the door he fancied that he heard his name. He turned and saw that Mr. Carey was beckoning him.

"Mr. Duff," said the dying man, his earnestness imparting a new vigour to his voice, "Mr. Duff, you have been speaking about Dr. Carey, Dr. Carey, Dr. Carey! When I am gone, say nothing about Dr. Carey — speak only of Dr. Carey's Savior."

Did I say that, when our little cobbler startled the cattle in the Northamptonshire lane, he was thinking only of the world, the world, *the world?* I was wrong! He was thinking primarily of the Savior, the Savior, *the Savior* — the *Savior* of the *World!*

And yet I was right; for the two visions are one vision, the two thoughts one thought.

The King, the King, the King!
The Continents, the Continents, the Continents!
The Savior, the Savior, the Savior!
The World, the World, the World!

As a lad, Carey caught the vision of *the King in His beauty;* and, as an inevitable consequence, he spent his life in the conquest of *the land that is very far off.*

12

THOMAS CHALMERS
(1780-1847)

Thomas Chalmers was one of the greatest Scottish preachers of his time. He was professor of moral philosophy at the University of St. Andrews and professor of theology at the University of Edinburgh.

He became pastor at Kilmany in 1803, but his preaching was ineffective until 1811, when he had an evangelical conversion. His preaching ministry underwent a remarkable change. He had an impressive work among the poor, was interested in charity work, and was successful in establishing Sunday schools. All those activities, however, were subservient to his pulpit ministry.

Chalmers became the leader of the Free Church of Scotland in 1843 when the state refused the right of a congregation to choose its own minister. He was also a mover of evangelism and revival in the church. The newly established Free Church organized a college in Edinburgh, and Chalmers became principal and a professor of the school.

His most famous sermons, perhaps, are his *Astronomical Discourses* and *The Expulsive Power of a New Affection.*

His text: "Believe on the Lord Jesus Christ, and thou shalt be saved" (Acts 16:31).

I

It was a mystery. Nobody in Kilmany could understand it. They were people of the flock and the field, men of the plough and the pasture. There were only about one hundred and fifty families scattered across the parish, and such social life as they enjoyed all circled around the kirk. They were all very fond of their young minister, and very proud of his distinguished academic attainments. Already, in his preaching, there were hints of that "sublime thunder" that afterwards rolled through the world. In his later years it was said of him that Scotland shuddered beneath his billowy eloquence as a cathedral vibrates to the deep notes of the organ. He became, as Lord Rosebery has testified, the most illustrious Scotsman since John Knox. But his farmer folk at Kilmany could not be expected to foresee all this. They felt that their minister was no ordinary man; yet there was one thing about him that puzzled every member of the congregation.

The drovers talked of it as they met each other on the long and lonely roads; the women discussed it as they waited outside the kirk while their husbands harnessed up the horses; the farmers themselves referred to it wonderingly when they talked things over in the stockyards and the market-place. Mr. Chalmers was only twenty-three. He had matriculated at twelve; had become a divinity student at fifteen; and at nineteen had been licensed to preach. Now that, with much fear and trembling, he had settled at Kilmany, he made a really excellent minister. He has himself told us that, as he rode about his parish, his affections flew before him. He loved to get to the firesides of the people, and he won from old and young their unstinted admiration, their confidence and their love. But for all that, the mystery remained.

Briefly stated, it was this: Why did he persist in preaching to these decent, well-meaning and law-abiding Scottish farmers in a strain that implied that they ought all to be in jail? Why, Sabbath after Sabbath, did he thunder at them concerning the heinous wickedness of theft, of murder, and of adultery? After a hard week's work in field and stable, byre and dairy, these sturdy Scotsmen drove to the kirk at the sound of the Sabbath bell, only to be berated by the minister as though they had spent the week in open shame! They filed into their family pews with their wives and their sons and their daughters, and were straightway charged with all the crimes in the calendar!

Later on, the minister himself saw both the absurdity and the pity of it. It was, as he told the good people of Kilmany, part of his bitter self-reproach that, for the greater part of the time he spent among them, "I could expatiate only on the meanness of dishonesty, on the villany of falsehood, on the despicable arts of calumny, in a word, upon all those deformities of character which awaken the natural indignation of the human heart against the pests and disturbers of human society."

Now and again, the brilliant and eloquent young preacher turned aside from this line of things in order to denounce the designs of Napoleon. But as the Fifeshire farmers saw no way in which the arguments of their minister were likely to come under the notice of the tyrant and turn him from his fell purpose of invading Britain, they were as much perplexed by these sermons as by the others. This kind of thing continued without a break from 1803 until 1811; and the parish stood bewildered.

II

From 1803 until 1811! But what of the four years that followed? For he remained at Kilmany until 1815 — the year of Waterloo! Let me set a second picture beside the one I have already painted! Could any contrast be greater? The people were bewildered before: they were even more bewildered now! The minister was another man: the kirk was another place! During those closing years at Kilmany, Mr. Chalmers thundered against the grosser crimes no more. He never again held forth from his pulpit against the iniquities of the Napoleonic program. But every Sunday he had something fresh to say about the love of God, about the Cross of Christ, and about the way of salvation. Every Sunday he urged his people with tears to repent, to believe, and to enter into life everlasting. Every Sunday he set before them the beauty of the Christian life, and, by all the arts of eloquent persuasion, endeavoured to lead his people into it. "He would bend over the pulpit," writes one who heard him both before and after the change, "he would bend over the pulpit and press us to take the gift, as if he held it that moment in his hand and would not be satisfied till every one of us had got possession of it. And often, when the sermon was over, and the psalm was sung, and he rose to pronounce the blessing, he would break out afresh with some new entreaty, unwilling to let us go until he had made one more effort to persuade us to accept it."

Now here are the two pictures of Chalmers during his last four years there! The question is: What happened in 1811 to bring about the change?

III

That is the question; and the answer, bluntly stated, is that, in 1811, Chalmers was converted! He made a startling discovery — the most sensational discovery that any man ever made. He had occupied all the years of his ministry on the Ten Commandments; he now discovered, not only that there are more commandments than ten, but that the greatest commandments of all are not to be found among the ten!

The experience of Chalmers resembles in many respects the experience of the Marquis of Lossie. Readers of George Macdonald's *Malcolm* will never forget the chapter on "The Marquis and the Schoolmaster." The dying marquis sends for the devout schoolmaster, Mr. Graham. The schoolmaster knows his man, and goes cautiously to work.

"Are you satisfied with yourself, my lord?"

"No, by God!"

"You would like to be better?"

"Yes; but how is a poor devil to get out of this infernal scrape?"

"Keep the commandments!"

"That's it, of course; but there's no time!"

"If there were but time to draw another breath, there would be time to begin!"

"How am I to begin? Which am I to begin with?"

"There is one commandment which includes all the rest!"

"Which is that?"

"Believe on the Lord Jesus Christ and thou shalt be saved!"

When the Marquis of Lossie passed from the ten commandments to the commandment that includes all the ten, he found the peace for which he hungered, and, strangely enough, Chalmers entered into life in a precisely similar way.

IV

"I am much taken," he says in his journal, in May, 1811, "I am much taken with Graham's observation that we are *commanded* to believe on the Son of God!"

Commanded!

The Ten Commandments!

The Commandment that includes all the Commandments!

"Believe on the Lord Jesus Christ and thou shalt be saved!"

That was the Marquis of Lossie's text, and it was Chalmers'.

At about this time, he was overtaken by a serious illness. He always regarded those days of feebleness and confinement as the critical days in his spiritual history. Long afterwards, when the experience of the years had shown that the impressions then made were not transitory, he wrote to his brother giving him an account of the change that then overtook him. He describes it as a great revolution in all his methods of thought. "I am now most thoroughly of opinion," he goes on, "that on the system of 'Do this and live!' no peace can ever be attained. It is *'Believe on the Lord Jesus Christ and thou shalt be saved!'* When this belief enters the heart, joy and confidence enter along with it!"

"Thus," says Dr. Hanna in his great biography of Chalmers, "thus we see him stepping from the treacherous ground of 'Do and live!' to place his feet upon the firm foundation of *'Believe on the Lord Jesus Christ and thou shalt be saved!'*"

Do! — The Ten Commandments — that was his theme at Kilmany for eight long years!

Believe! — The Commandment that includes all the Commandments — that was the word that transformed his life and transfigured his ministry!

"Believe on the Lord Jesus Christ and thou shalt be saved!"

V

The result of that change we have partly seen. But only partly. We have seen it from the point of view of *the pew*. We have seen the farmer-folk of Kilmany astonished as they caught a new note in the minister's preaching, a new accent in the minister's voice. But we must see the change from the point of view of *the pulpit*. And, as seen from the pulpit, the result of the transformation was even more surprising and sensational. Chalmers alone can tell that story, and we must let him tell it in his own way.

The twelve years at Kilmany — the eight *before* the change, and the four *after* it — have come to an end at last; and, at a special meeting called for the purpose, Mr. Chalmers is taking a sorrowful farewell of his first congregation. The farmers and their wives have driven in from far and near. Their minister has been called to a great city charge; they are proud of it; but they find it hard to give him up. The valedictory speeches have all been made, and now Mr. Chalmers rises to reply. After a feeling acknowledgement of the compliments paid him, he utters one of the most impressive and valuable testimonies to which any minister ever gave expression.

"I cannot but record," he says, "the effect of an actual though undesigned experiment which I prosecuted for upwards of twelve years among you. For the first eight years of that time I could expatiate only on the meanness of dishonesty, on the villany of falsehood, on the despicable arts of calumny, in a word, upon all those deformities of character which awaken the natural indignation of the human heart against the pests and disturbers of human society. But the interesting fact is, that, during the whole of that period, I never once heard of any reformation being wrought amongst my people. All the vehemence with which I urged the virtues and the proprieties of social life had not the weight of a feather on the moral habits of my parishioners. It was not until the free offer of forgiveness through the blood of Christ was urged upon the acceptance of my hearers that I ever heard of any of those subordinate reformations which I made the ultimate object of my earlier ministrations."

And he closes that farewell speech with these memorable words: "You have taught me," he says, "that to preach Christ is the only effective way of preaching morality; and out of your humble cottages I have gathered a lesson which, in all its simplicity, I shall carry into a wider theater."

Do! — The Ten Commandments — that was his theme at Kilmany for eight long years, and it had not the weight of a feather!

Believe! — The Commandment that includes all the Commandments — that was his theme for the last four years, and he beheld its gracious and renovating effects in every home in the parish!

"Believe on the Lord Jesus Christ and thou shalt be saved!"

With that great witness on his lips, Chalmers lays down his charge at Kilmany, and plunges into a larger sphere to make world history!

VI

"Believe on the Lord Jesus Christ and thou shalt be saved!" Chalmers greatly believed and was greatly saved. He was saved from all sin and made saintly. "If ever a halo surrounded a saint," declares Lord Rosebery, "it encompassed Chalmers!" He was saved from all littleness and made great.

Mr. Gladstone used to say of him that the world can never forget "his warrior grandeur, his unbounded philanthropy, his strength of purpose, his mental integrity, his absorbed and absorbing earnestness; and, above all, his singular simplicity; he was one of nature's nobles."

"A strong-featured man," said Carlyle, thinking of the massive form, the leonine head, and the commanding countenance of his old friend; "a strong-featured man, and of very beautiful character."

When I want a definition of the salvation that comes by faith, I like to think of Thomas Chalmers.

VII

Yes, he greatly believed and was greatly saved; he greatly lived and greatly died. It is a Sunday evening. He — now an old man of sixty-seven — has remained at home, and has spent a delightful evening with his children and grandchildren. It is one of the happiest evenings that they have ever spent together. "We had family worship this morning," the old doctor says to a minister who happens to be present, "but you must give us worship again this evening. I expect to give worship in the morning!"

Immediately after prayers he withdraws, smiling and waving his hands to them all and wishing them "a general goodnight!"

They call him in the morning: but there is no response. *"I expect to give worship in the morning!"* he had said; and he has gone to give it! He is sitting up in bed, half erect, his head reclining gently on the pillow; the expression of his countenance that of fixed and majestic repose. His students liked to think that their old master had been translated at the zenith of his powers: he felt no touch of senile decay.

"Believe on the Lord Jesus Christ and thou shalt be saved!" What is it to be saved? I do not know. No man knows. But as I think of the transformation that the text effected in the experience of Chalmers; as I contemplate his valiant and unselfish life; together with his beautiful and glorious death; and as I try to conceive of the felicity into which that Sunday night he entered, I can form an idea.

13

ADONIRAM JUDSON

(1788-1850)

Adoniram Judson's father was a strict and domineering Congregational minister in Massachusetts. His mother was a gentlewoman, "polished in speech." Young Adoniram was brilliant, proper, proud, cultured, and refined. He learned navigation at ten, mastered Greek at twelve, and entered the university at sixteen. His aim was to be first in everything. He had visions of being an orator, a statesman, a man of wealth. In his dreaming of success, the thought occured to him — when he reached the top, where could he go from there?

God had different plans for Adoniram Judson. His life was dramatically changed when, at the age of twenty-one, he received Christ as Savior. Not long after this, he was given a book, *The Star of the East,* written by Claude Buchanan, chaplain of the British East India Company, which told how heathen lives had been transformed through the gospel. Even though he had been later offered the biggest church in Boston, he set sail for India and Burma, where he served his wonderful Lord until his death.

In Malden, Massachusetts, is an unimpressive marble tablet that reads:

In Memoriam
Rev. Adoniram Judson
Born August 9, 1788
Died April 12, 1850
Malden his birthplace
The Ocean his sepulchre
Converted Burmans and
The Burman Bible
His monument
His record is on High

His text: "To comprehend . . . what is the breadth, and length, and depth, and height; and to know the love of Christ" (Ephesians 3:18-19).

I

He is a thorough-paced sceptic, this dashing young fellow with the slight and fragile frame, the round and rosy face, the laughing brown eyes, and the rich shock of chestnut hair. There is something defiant about his unbelief. He is the son of a Congregational minister in Massachusetts, who cherishes a fond and secret hope of seeing his brilliant boy following in his own footsteps. But the son knows better than the sire. At school and at college he has swept everything before him. His teachers have stood astonished at the ease and splendor of his triumphs. In every classical contest, Adoniram Judson was first and his rivals nowhere.

His phenomenal success has awakened within him a proud and all-absorbing self-consciousness. The conquests that his dazzling intellectual endowments must win for him in the golden future fire his fancy with excited dreams. "Day and night," as one of his biographers puts it, "he feeds his ambition with visions of eminence and glory such as no mortal has yet won. Now he is a second Homer, thrilling a nation with heroic plays; now a mighty statesman, guiding, with steady hand, the destinies of his country; but, whatever the dream of the moment, its nucleus is ever his own transcendent greatness." A minister! *He* a Congregational minister! He smiles disdainfully at his father's lack of imagination.

This was in 1803; and in 1803 the hectic and amazing vogue of Tom Paine was at its very height. In every seat of learning it was considered the correct thing to pooh-pooh Christianity. It is said that, at Yale, every student was an avowed infidel. The graduates even adopted the names of the great French and English atheists, and asked to be addressed by those names in preference to their own.

The imperious mind of Judson was swiftly infected by the prevailing epidemic. At Providence College, in the class above his own, was a young fellow name E_____, a youth of rare genius, of sparkling wit, of high culture, and of charming personality. This senior student was powerfully attracted to Judson, and Judson was flattered and fascinated by his friendship. E_____ was, however, one of the leaders of the new philosophy; and, in accepting his companionship and confidence, Judson committed himself irretrievably to an attitude of audacious and aggressive unbelief. In those days his father's dreams of ordination seemed to rest upon a singularly flimsy foundation.

II

But, as is so often the case, it was the unexpected that happened. Wherever Adoniram Judson went, in the course of his historic and adventurous career, he carried with him, as Dr. Angus says, that evident of the truth of Christianity which is at once the most portable and the most conclusive — the vivid memory of a startling and sensational conversion.

Our sceptical young student makes up his mind to set out on horseback on a tour of the northern states. He rests one night at a certain wayside inn. The landlord explains apologetically that the only room that he can offer is one that adjoins an apartment in which a young man is lying very ill — dying, perhaps. Judson assures the innkeeper that it does not matter; death, he declares, is nothing to him; and, except that he will feel a natural sympathy for the unfortunate sufferer, the circumstance will in no way disturb him.

The partition between the two rooms is, however, terribly thin. In the stillness of the night, Judson lies awake, listening to the groans of the dying man — groans of anguish; groans, he sometimes fancies, of despair. The heartrending sounds powerfully affect him. But he pulls himself together. What would his college companions say if *they* knew of his weakness? And, above all, what would the clear-minded, highly-intellectual, sparklingly-witty E——— say? How, after feeling as he had felt, could he look into the face of E——— again? But it is of no use. The awful sounds in the next room continue, and although he hides his head beneath the blankets, he hears everything — and shudders! At length, however, all is still. He rises at dawn; seeks the innkeeper; and inquires about his neighbor.

"He's dead!" is the blunt reply.

"Dead!" replies Judson. "And who was he?"

"Oh," explains the innkeeper languidly, "he was a student from Providence College; a very fine fellow; his name was E———!"

Judson is completely stunned. He feels that he cannot continue his tour. He turns his horse's head towards his old home;

opens his stricken heart to his father and mother; and begs them to help him to a faith that will stand the test of life and of death, of time and of eternity. Full of the thoughts that his parents suggest to him, he retires to the calm seclusion of Andover, and there, with nothing to distract his attention from the stupendous themes that are pressing upon his mind, he makes a solemn dedication of himself to God. He feels, beyond the shadow of a doubt, that he has become a new creature in Christ Jesus. Returning home, he gladdens everybody by announcing his momentous decision; and, in the year that marks his coming of age, he becomes a member of his father's Church.

During these memorable days of crisis and of consecration one overwhelming thought has taken possession of his mind. *The love of Christ!* The love that, in the days of his overweening pride and selfish ambition, had not cast him off; the love that had neither been estranged by his waywardness nor alienated by his blatant and audacious unbelief; the love that had followed him everywhere; the love that would not let him go! Here, on my desk, are three separate accounts of his conversion. In summing up the situation, each writer refers to this factor in the case.

"*The love of Christ* displaced selfish ambition as the ruling motive of his life," says the first.

"He became a man of one idea — *the love of Christ* — and he desired to spend his whole life in demonstrating it," says the second.

"Having been forgiven much, *he loved much,*" says the third.

To comprehend the breadth and length and depth and height and to know the love of Christ which passeth knowledge — this became, at the dawn of his manhood, his one supreme and passionate aspiration. It is the climax of all that has gone before; it is the key of all that follows.

III

The depth and height of the love of Christ — he knew something of the *depths* from which it could rescue, and of the *heights* to which it could raise.

But *the breadth and length of the love of Christ* — here was a new conception! The *breadth* and *length!* It seemed to embrace the whole wide world! And yet the world knew nothing of it! The idea took such a hold upon his mind that he could think of nothing else. He was haunted by the visions of nations dying in the dark. He started in his sleep at the thought of India, of Africa, and of China. The situation so appalled him that he became incapable of study. Then, one never-to-be-forgotten day, as he was taking a solitary walk in the woods, it seemed to him that the Savior Himself drew near and said: *"Go ye into all the world and preach the gospel to every creature."* His course was clear! Come wind, come weather, he must go!

But how? There was no Mission Board or Missionary Society to which he could apply. He talked it over with his fellow students until half a dozen of them were as eager as himself for such service. They petitioned the heads of the denomination, who, in their perplexity, laid the matter before the Churches. To the surprise of everybody, money poured in, and the newly-formed committee was able to equip the mission party, advancing each man a whole year's salary. Before leaving his native land, Judson had married. He and his bride sailed from Salem on February 18, 1812; they were welcomed at Calcutta by William Carey four months later; and, after a brief stay, set out for Burma. They reached Rangoon in July 1813. Their first home was a rude hut built on a swamp outside the city wall. Wild beasts prowled around it. Near by, to the left, was the pit into which the offal of the city was poured. Near by, to the right, was the place where the bodies of the dead were burned. The young couple were sickened and disgusted by every sight and smell. On the day of their arrival, poor Mrs. Judson was too ill to walk or ride; she had to be carried to her unalluring home. Yet there was no repining. Both husband and wife smiled at the primitive conditions under which their first home was established; and, with brave hearts, they solemnly engaged to spend their entire lives among their barbarous and inhospitable neighbors.

IV

And they kept their word, although the price they had to pay was terrible beyond words. On one occasion we see Mr. Judson, starved to a skeleton, being driven in chains across the burning desert, until, his back bleeding beneath the lash and his feet blistered by the hot sand, he sinks, utterly exhausted, to the ground and prays for the merciful relief of a speedy death.

On another occasion he is imprisoned for nearly two years in a foul and noisome den, his confinement being embittered by every device that a barbarous and malignant brutality could invent. He must have sunk under the fierce ordeal had not Mrs. Judson, often under cover of darkness, crept to the door of his horrid cell and ministered to him. For three weeks, it is true, she absented herself from the prison; but, when she returned, she bore a little child in her arms to explain her delinquency. Shortly afterwards the mission-house was stripped of every comfort; Mrs. Jusdon is left without even a chair or seat of any kind. To add to her troubles, Mary, her elder child, develops small-pox. Under the terrific strain, the poor mother finds herself unable to nurse her baby, and its pitiful cries intensify her anguish. In sheer desperation, she bribes the jailers to release her husband for an hour or two. And, while *she* applies herself to the little patient who is tossing in the delirium of the dreaded scourge, *he* carries the baby into the village, begging the nursing-mothers there to pity and nourish it.

The crisis passes; but passes to be followed by others. It was announced that Mr. Judson's imprisonment was to be terminated by his execution. The exact date and hour were proclaimed; and the husband and wife braced themselves for the tragic separation. In the interval, however, he was smuggled away, and the distracted wife had no inkling as to what had become of him. And one of the most pitiful and pathetic pages in the annals of Christian missions is the page that describes the subsequent return of Mr. Judson to his stricken home. *He* was scarred, maimed, and emaciated by long suffering; *she* was so worn and haggard that he could scarcely recognize her. Her glossy black curls had all been shaved from her finely-shaped head. She was dressed in rags — the only garments left her — and everything about her told of extreme wretchedness and privation.

And, before he had been fourteen years in Burma, he had buried his wife and all his children there. Yet, through it all, he never for a moment doubted the reality and richness of *the love of Christ.*

"*The love of Christ!*" he says again and again in his letters, "*the breadth and length and depth and height of the love of Christ!* If I had not felt certain that every additional trial was ordered by infinite love and mercy, I could not have survived my accumulated sufferings."

V

But there were joys as well as sorrows. That was a great and golden day on which, after six long years of diligent labor, he welcomed his first convert. He never forgot the emotions with which, that day, he and Mrs. Judson took the Communion with a son of the soil who had entered into a deep and transforming realization of the wonder of the love of Christ.

On that day he set before himself two lofty aims. He prayed that he might live to translate the entire Bible into the native language, and to preside over a native Church of at least one hundred members. He more than realized both ambitions. He not only translated the whole Bible into the Burman tongue, but wrote, in addition, many valuable pamphlets in the native language. And, before he had been twenty years in Burma, he had baptized his hundredth convert. After more than thirty years he revisited his native land.

"Behold," exclaimed the chairman of the great meeting that welcomed him at Richmond, Virginia, "behold what a change God hath wrought in Burma! The entire Bible has been skilfully translated, carefully revised, accurately printed, and eagerly read. In a land so recently enveloped in darkness and superstition, many vigorous Churches have been planted. Native preachers have been raised up to proclaim, in their own tongue, and among their own people, the unsearchable riches of Christ. The Karens, a simple-hearted and singular people, are turning by hundreds and thousands to the Lord. Among them the gospel has met with a success rarely equalled since the days of the apostles. On Burma the morning light is breaking!"

And, in achieving these notable triumphs, Mr. Judson adhered constantly to his old theme. *"Think much on the love of Christ!"* he used to say to all his converts and inquirers, "think much on *the love of Christ!"* He seemed convinced, as Dr. Wayland says, that the whole world could be converted if only each separate individual could be persuaded that there was a place for him in the divine love.

VI

"Think much on *the love of Christ!"* It was the keynote of all his days. He returned to his beloved Burma; but he was never quite the same again. His health was shattered and his strength was spent. It was clear that his time was short. But in one respect, at least, he was unchanged. He talked with even greater fervor, frequency, and fondness of the deathless love of his Lord. "And," adds his biographer, "if he found anything clouding his con-sciousness and enjoyment of *the love of Christ*, he would go away into the jungle and live there by himself until the sweetness of his faith had been restored to him."

He died at sea. In the course of that last voyage, undertaken in search of health, he harped continually on the one familiar string. Mr. Thomas Ranney, who accompanied him, says that he kept repeating one text: *"As I have loved you, so ought ye to love one another." "As I have loved you,"* he would exclaim; *"as I have loved you!"* and then he would cry ecstatically: "Oh, the love of Christ! *The love of Christ!"*

Later, when confined to his berth, he would talk of nothing else. "Oh, the love of Christ! *The love of Christ!"* he would mur-mur, his eyes kindling with enthusiasm and the tears chasing each other down his cheeks. *"The love of Christ — its breadth and length and depth and height —* we cannot comprehend it now — but what a study for eternity!" And, even after he had lost the power of speech, his lips still framed in silence the familiar syllables: *"The love of Christ! The love of Christ!"*

A few days before he passed, he spoke, with evident pleasure, of being buried at sea. It gave, he said, a sense of freedom and expansion; it contrasted agreeably with the dark and narrow grave to which he had committed so many whom he loved. The vast blue ocean, into which his body was lowered a day or two later, seemed to his dying fancy a symbol of his Savior's un-fathomable and boundless love — the love that passeth knowl-edge — the love that knows neither measure nor end, neither sounding or shore.

14

DAVID LIVINGSTONE
(1813-1873)

For more than thirty years David Livingstone gave his life to missionary work, to stamp out slave trade, and to open up Africa to civilization and commerce.

Livingstone was accepted by the London Missionary Society as a medical missionary to China. Because of the Opium War there, the society sent him to South Africa in 1840 to work with Robert Moffat. He soon became convinced that efforts should be made as soon as possible to reach the teeming African tribespeople in the interior with the gospel, and he lost no time in opening new stations.

David Livingstone will be remembered as an explorer because of his famous statement made in 1853, "I shall open up a path into the interior or perish." However, in a letter to his father he wrote, "I am a missionary, heart and soul. God had an only Son, and He was a missionary and a physician. A poor, poor imitation of Him I am, or wish to be. In this service I hope to live; in it I wish to die."

Largely through Livingstone's efforts, the continent was opened both to missions and to civilization. His discoveries are still being explored today.

His African servants found David Livingstone dead, kneeling by his bedside as if in prayer, on May 1, 1873, in a village in Zambia. His heart was buried in Africa, but his body was taken to England and buried in Westminster Abbey on April 4, 1874.

His text: "Lo, I am with you alway, even unto the end of the world" (Matthew 28:20).

I

"It is the word of a gentleman of the most strict and sacred honor, so there's an end of it!" says Livingstone to himself as he places his finger for the thousandth time on the text on which he stakes his life. He is surrounded by hostile and infuriated savages. During the sixteen years that he has spent in Africa, he has never before seemed in such imminent peril. Death stares him in the face. He thinks sadly of his life-work scarcely begun. For the first time in his experience he is tempted to steal away under cover of the darkness and to seek safety in flight. He prays! "Leave me not, forsake me not!" he cries. But let me quote from his own journal: it will give us the rest of the story.

"January 14, 1856. Evening. Felt much turmoil of spirit in prospect of having all my plans for the welfare of this great region and this teeming population knocked on the head by savages tomorrow. But I read that Jesus said: 'All power is given unto Me in heaven and in earth. Go ye therefore, and teach all nations, and *lo, I am with you alway, even unto the end of the world.'* It is the word of a gentleman of the most strict and sacred honor, so there's an end of it! I will not cross furtively tonight as I intended. Should such a man as I flee? Nay, verily, I shall take observations for latitude and longitude tonight, though they may be the last. I feel quite calm now, thank God!"

The words in italics are underlined in the journal, and they were underlined in his heart. Later in the same year, he pays his first visit to the Homeland. Honors are everywhere heaped upon him. The University of Glasgow confers upon him the degree of Doctor of Laws. On such occasions the recipient of the honor is usually subjected to some banter at the hands of the students. But when Livingstone rises, bearing upon his person the marks of his struggles and sufferings in darkest Africa, he is received in reverential silence. He is gaunt and haggard as a result of his long exposure to the tropical sun. On nearly thirty occasions he has been laid low by the fevers that steam from the inland swamps, and these severe illnesses have left their mark. His left arm, crushed by a lion, hangs helplessly at his side. A hush falls upon the great assembly as he announces his resolve to return to the land for which he has already endured so much.

"But I return," he says, "without misgiving and with great gladness. For would you like me to tell you what supported me through all the years of exile among people whose language I could not understand, and whose attitude towards me was always uncertain and often hostile? It was this: *'Lo, I am with you alway, even unto the end of the world!'* On those words I staked everything, and they never failed!"

"Leave me not, forsake me not!" he prays.

"Lo, I am with you alway, even unto the end of the world!" comes the response.

"It is the word of a gentleman of the most strict and sacred honor, so there's an end of it!" he tells himself.

On that pledge he hazarded his all. And it did not fail him.

II

When, I wonder, did David Livingstone first make that text his own? I do not know. It must have been very early. He used to say that he never had any difficulty in carrying with him his father's portrait because, in "The Cottar's Saturday Night," Robert Burns had painted it for him. Down to the last morning that he spent in his old home at Blantyre, the household joined in family worship. It was still dark when they knelt down that bleak November morning. They are up at five. The mother makes the coffee: the father prepares to walk with his boy to Glasgow; and David himself leads the household to the Throne of Grace. The thought embedded in his text is uppermost in his mind. He is leaving those who are dearer to him than life itself; yet there is One on whose Presence he can still rely. *"Lo, I am with you alway, even unto the end of the world!"*

And so, in selecting the passage to be read by lamplight in the little kitchen on this memorable morning, David selects the Psalm that, more clearly than any other, promises him, on every sea and on every shore, the Presence of the Lord. *"The Lord is thy keeper. The sun shall not smite thee by day, nor the moon by night. The Lord shall preserve thee from all evil: He shall preserve thy soul. The Lord shall preserve thy going out and thy coming in from this time forth, and even for evermore."* After prayers comes the anguish of farewell. But the ordeal is softened for them all by the thought that has been suggested by David's reading and by David's prayer.

In the grey light of that wintry morning, father and son set out on their long and cheerless tramp. I remember, years ago, standing on the Broomielaw, on the spot that witnessed their parting. I could picture the elder man turning sadly back towards his Lanarkshire home, while David hurried off to make his final preparations for sailing. But, deeper than their sorrow, there is in each of their hearts a song — the song of the Psalm they have read together in the kitchen — the song of the Presence — the song of the text!

"Leave me not, forsake me not!" cries the lonely lad.

"Lo, I am with you alway, even unto the end of the world!"

"It is the word of a gentleman of the most strict and sacred honor, so there's an end of it!"

And with that song singing itself in his soul, David Livingstone turns his face towards darkest Africa.

III

If ever a man needed a comrade, David Livingstone did. Apart from that divine companionship, his is the most lonely life in history. It is doubtless good for the world that most men are content to marry and settle down, to weave about themselves the web of domestic felicity, to face each day the task that lies nearest to them, and to work out their destiny without worrying about the remote and the unexplored. But it is equally good for the world that there are a few adventurous spirits in every age who feel themselves taunted and challenged and dared by the mystery of the great unknown. As long as there is a pole undiscovered, a sea uncharted, a forest untracked or a desert uncrossed, they are restless and ill at ease. It is the most sublime form that curiosity assumes.

From the moment of his landing on African soil, Livingstone is haunted, night and day, by the visions that beckon and the voices that call from out of the undiscovered. For his poor wife's sake he tries hard, and tries repeatedly, to settle down to the life of an ordinary mission station. But it is impossible. The lure of the wilds fascinates him. He sees, away on the horizon, the smoke of a thousand native settlements in which no white man has ever been seen. It is more than he can bear. He goes to some of them and beholds, on arrival, the smoke of yet other settlements still farther away.

And so he wanders further and further from his starting point; and builds home after home, only to desert each home as soon as it is built! The tales that the natives tell him of vast inland seas and of wild tumultuous waters tantalize him beyond endurance.

The instincts of the hydrographer tingle within him. He sees the three great rivers — the Nile, the Congo, and the Zambesi — emptying themselves into three separate oceans, and he convinces himself that the man who can solve the riddle of their sources will have opened up a continent to the commerce and civilization of the world. The treasures of history present us with few things more affecting than the hold this ambition secures upon his heart.

It lures him on and on — along the tortuous slavetracks littered everywhere with bones — through the long grass that stands up like a wall on either side of him — across the swamps, the marshes, and the bogs of the watersheds — through forests dark as night and through deserts that no man has ever crossed before — on and on for more than thirty thousand miles. He makes a score of discoveries, any one of which would have established his fame; but none of these satisfy him. The unknown still calls loudly and will not be denied.

Even at the last, worn to a shadow, suffering in every limb, and too feeble to put his feet to the ground, the mysterious fountains of Herodotus torture his fancy. "The fountains!" he murmurs in his delirium, "the hidden fountains!" And with death stamped upon his face, he orders his faithful blacks to bear him on a rude litter in his tireless search for the elusive streams.

Yet never once does he feel really lonely. One has but to read his journal in order to see that that word of stainless honor never failed him. The song that soothed and comforted the weeping household in the Blantyre kitchen cheered with its music the hazards and adventures of his life in Africa.

"Leave me not, forsake me not!"

"Lo, I am with you alway, even unto the end of the world!"

"It is the word of a gentleman of the most strict and sacred honor, so there's an end of it!"

Thus, amidst savages and solitudes, Livingstone finds that great word grandly true.

IV

"It is His word of honor!" says Livingstone; and, nothing if not practical, he straightway proceeds to act upon it. "If He be with me, I can do anything, *anything, anything!*" It is the echo of another apostolic boast: "I can do all things through Christ that strengtheneth me!" In that unwavering confidence, and with an

audacity that is the best evidence of his faith, Livingstone draws up for himself a program so colossal that it would still have seemed large had it been the project of a million men. *"It is His word of honor!"* he reasons; "and if He will indeed be with me, even unto the end, He and I can accomplish what a million men, unattended by the Divine Companion, would tremble to attempt." And so, he draws up with a calm hand and a fearless heart that prodigious program from which he never for a moment swerved, and which, when all was over, was inscribed upon his tomb in Westminster Abbey. Relying on "the word of a gentleman of the most strict and sacred honor," he sets himself —

1. *To evangelize the native races*
2. *To explore the undiscovered secrets*
3. *To abolish the desolating slave trade*

Some men set themselves to evangelize; some make it their business to explore; others feel called to emancipate; but Livingstone, with a golden secret locked up in his heart, undertakes all three!

Evangelization!
Exploration!
Emancipation!

Those were his watchwords. No man ever set himself a more tremendous task: no man ever confronted his lifework with a more serene and joyous confidence!

V

And how did it all work out? Was his faith justified? Was that *word of honor* strictly kept?

"Leave me not, forsake me not!" he cries.

"Lo, I am with you alway, even unto the end!"

In spite of that assurance, did he ever find himself a solitary in a strange and savage land? Was he ever left or forsaken? It sometimes looked like it.

It looked like it when he stood, bent with anguish beside that sad and lonely grave at Shupanga. Poor Mary Livingstone — the daughter of Robert and Mary Moffat — was never strong enough to be the constant companion of a pioneer. For years she struggled on through dusty deserts and trackless jungles, seeing no other woman but the wild women about her. But, with little children at her skirts, she could not struggle on for long. She gave it up, and stayed at home to care for the bairns and to pray for her husband as he pressed tirelessly on.

But, even in Africa, people will talk. The gossips at the white settlements were incapable of comprehending any motive that could lead a man to leave his wife and plunge into the interior, save the desire to be as far from her as possible. Hearing of the scandal, and stung by it, Livingstone, in a weak moment, sent for his wife to again join him. She came; she sickened; and she died.

We have all been touched by that sad scene in the vast African solitude. We seem to have seen him sitting beside the rude bed, formed of boxes covered with a soft mattress, on which lies his dying wife. The man who has faced so many deaths, and braved so many dangers, is now utterly broken down. He weeps like a child. "Oh, my Mary, my Mary!" he cries, as the gentle spirit sighs itself away, "I loved you when I married you, and, the longer I lived with you, I loved you the more! How often we have longed for a quiet home since you and I were cast adrift in Africa! God pity the poor children!" He buries her under the large baobab tree, sixty feet in circumference, and reverently marks her grave. "For the first time in my life," he says, "I feel willing to die! I am left alone in the world by one whom I felt to be a part of myself!"

"Leave me not, forsake me not!" he cried at the outset.

"I am left alone!" he cries in his anguish now.

Has the *word of honor* been violated? Has it? It certainly looks like it!

VI

It looked like it, too, eleven years later, when his own time came. He is away up among the bogs and the marshes near Chitambo's village in Ilala. Save only for his native helpers, he is all alone. He is all alone, and at the end of everything. He walked as long as he could walk; rode as long as he could ride; and was carried on a litter as long as he could bear it.

But now, with his feet too ulcerated to bear the touch of the ground; with his frame so emaciated that it frightens him when he sees it in the glass; and with a horrible inward hemorrhage draining away his scanty remnant of vitality, he can go no further. "Knocked up quite!" he says, in the last indistinct entry in his journal. A drizzling rain is falling, and the black men hastily build a hut to shelter him. In his fever, he babbles about the fountains, the sources of the rivers, the undiscovered streams. Two of the black boys, almost as tired as their master, go to rest, appointing a third to watch the sick man's bed.

But he, too, sleeps. And when he wakes, in the cold grey of the dawn, the vision that confronts him fills him with terror. The white man is not in bed, but on his knees beside it! He runs and awakens his two companions. They creep timidly to the kneeling figure. It is cold and stiff! Their great master is dead! No white man near! No woman's hand to close his eyes in that last cruel sickness! No comrade to fortify his faith with the deathless words of everlasting comfort and everlasting hope! He dies alone!

"Leave me not; forsake me not!" he cried at the beginning.

"He died alone!" — that is how it all ended!

Has the *word of honor* been violated? It most certainly looks like it!

VII

But it only *looks* like it! Life is full of illusions, and so is death. Any one who cares to read the records in the journal of that terrible experience at Shupanga will be made to feel that never for a moment did the *word of honor* really fail.

"Lo, I am with you alway, even unto the end!"

The consciousness of that unfailing Presence was his one source of comfort as he sat by his wife's bedside and dug her grave. The assurance of that divine Presence was the one heartening inspiration that enabled him to take up his heavy burden and struggle on again!

"Lo, I am with you alway, even unto the end!"

Yes, even unto the end! Take just one more peep at the scene in the hut at Chitambo's village. He died on his knees! Then to whom was he talking when he died? He was talking, even to the last moment of his life, to the constant Companion of his long, long pilgrimage! He was speaking, even in the act and article of death, to that "Gentleman of the most strict and sacred honor" whose word he had so implicitly trusted.

"He will keep His word" — it is among the last entries in his journal — "He will keep His word, the Gracious one, full of grace and truth; no doubt of it. He will keep His word, and it will be all right. Doubt is here inadmissable, surely!"

"Leave me not; forsake me not!" he cried at the beginning.

"Lo, I am with you alway, even unto the end!" came the assuring response.

"It is the word of a gentleman of the most strict and sacred honor, so there's an end of it!"

And that pathetic figure on his knees is the best testimony to the way in which that sacred pledge was kept.

15

CATHERINE BOOTH
(1829-1890)

Catherine Booth is often called the "mother of the Salvation Army." She and her husband, William, were excommunicated from the Wesleyan Church in England along with a group of "reformers." The Booths then broke away from the "reformers" and began a missionary work in East London among the poor, lower classes. This work gradually developed into the Salvation Army.

Catherine Booth defended the right of women to preach in public. She delivered the first sermon in her husband's pulpit. She conducted a series of meetings throughout England until she was stricken with cancer. She died two years later after great suffering.

Her text: "My grace is sufficient for thee" (2 Corinthians 12:9).

I

Who that was in London on October 14, 1890, can forget the extraordinary scenes that marked the funeral of Catherine Booth? It was a day of universal grief. The whole nation mourned. For Mrs. Booth was one of the most striking personalities, and one of the mightiest spiritual forces, of the nineteenth century. To the piety of a Saint Teresa she added the passion of a Josephine Butler, the purposefulness of an Elizabeth Fry, and the practical sagacity of a Frances Willard.

The greatest in the land revered her, trusted her, consulted her, deferred to her. The letters that passed between Catherine

Booth and Queen Victoria are among the most remarkable documents in the literature of correspondence. Mr. Gladstone attached the greatest weight to her judgment and convictions. Bishop Lightfoot, one of the most distinguished scholars of his time, has testified to the powerful influence which she exerted over him. And while the loftiest among men honored her, the lowliest loved her.

Such strong lives have their secrets. Mrs. Booth had hers. Her secret was *a text*. As a child she learned it by heart; as a girl she pinned her faith to the promise it enshrined; amidst the stress and strain of a stormy and eventful life she trusted it implicitly; and, with all the tenacity of her keen, clear intellect, she clung to it at the last. In the standard *Life of Catherine Booth* — a huge work of a thousand pages — four chapters are devoted to the scenes at the deathbed. And then we read:

"The lips moved as though desiring to speak. Unable, however, to do so, the dying woman pointed to a wall-text, which had for a long time been placed opposite to her, so that her eyes could rest upon it.

MY GRACE
IS
SUFFICIENT FOR THEE.

It was taken down and placed near her on the bed. But it was no longer needed. The promise had been completely fulfilled."

"That," said a speaker at one of the Great Memorial Meetings in London, some of which were attended by many thousand people, "that was her text!" And, as so often happens, her text explains her character.

For, considered apart from the text, the character is an insoluble enigma. It is like a consequence without a cause. I was talking a week or two ago with an old man, who, in Australia's earlier days, did a good deal of pioneering in the heart of the bush.

"Once," he told me, "soon after I first came out, I really thought that I had reached the end of everything. I was hopelessly lost. My strength was utterly exhausted. I had gone as far as I could go. The country around me was flat and dry; my thirst was a perfect agony; and my poor dog followed at my heels, her tongue hanging out, and her sides panting pitifully. We had not seen water for several days. I sat down under a great gum tree, hoping that an hour's rest would bring me fresh heart and new vigor. I must have fallen asleep. When I awoke, Fan was standing near me, wagging her tail. She seemed contented and satisfied; her tongue no longer protruded. An hour or two later, I suddenly missed her; she had vanished in the scrub. I determined to watch her. Presently she set out again, and I followed. Surely enough, she had found a tiny spring in a slight hollow about a half a mile away; and by that spring we were saved."

I have seen something like this in a higher realm. I recall, for example, Richard Cecil's story of his conversion. Richard Cecil — the friend and biographer of John Newton — was one of the great evangelical forces of the *eighteenth* century, as Catherine Booth was of the *nineteenth*. But, in his early days, Richard Cecil was a sceptic. He called himself an infidel, but he was honest in his infidelity. He could face facts; and the man who can look facts fairly in the face is not far from the kingdom of God. Richard Cecil was not, his scepticism notwithstanding. "I see," he says, in telling us of the line of thought that he pursued as he lay in bed one night, "I see two unquestionable facts." And what were they? They both concerned his mother.

"*First*, my mother is greatly afflicted in circumstances, body and mind; and I see that she cheerfully bears up under all her suffering by the support that she derives from constantly retiring to her quiet room and her Bible.

"*Second*, my mother has a secret spring of comfort of which I know nothing; while I, who give an unbounded loose to my appetites, and seek pleasure by every means, seldom or never find it. If, however, there is any secret in religion, why may I not attain to it as well as my mother? I will immediately seek it!"

He did; and those who are familiar with his life story know of the triumphant result of that quest. It was precisely so with Mrs. Booth. Her children knew that, like the bushman's collie, she found refreshment at some secret spring. Later on, she told them of the text and led them, one by one, to the fountains of grace. *"My grace is sufficient for thee."* And when, at last, the avenues of speech and hearing were closed, they hung the golden words before her clouding eyes. Again she greeted them with rapture, and, with unwavering confidence, pointed her children to their deathless message.

II

In his *Grace Abounding*, John Bunyan tells us that there was a period in his spiritual history when his soul was like a pair of scales. It partook of three phases. At one time the right-hand balance was down and the left-hand empty and high; then for a while they were exactly and evenly poised; and, at the last, the left-hand balance dropped and that on the right hand was swinging in the air.

At the *first* of these stages he was being tormented about the unpardonable sin. He reminded himself that, for Esau, there was no place for repentance; and he felt that there was none for him. The scale in which he laid his despair was heavily weighted; the scale in which he placed his hope was empty!

And the *second* stage — the stage that levelled the balances? "One morning," he says, "as I was at prayer, and trembling with fear, lest there should be no word of God to help me, that piece of a sentence darted in upon me: *My grace is sufficient!* At this I felt some stay as if there might yet be hope. About a fortnight before, I had been looking at this very scripture, but I then thought that it could bring me no comfort, and I threw down the book in a pet. I thought that the grace was not large enough for me! no, not large enough! But now it was as if the arms of grace were so wide that they could enclose not only me but many more besides. And so *this* about the sufficiency of grace and *that* about Esau finding no place for repentance would be like a pair of scales within my mind. Sometimes one end would be uppermost and sometimes again the other; according to which would be my peace or trouble."

And the *third* stage — the triumphant stage? Bunyan felt that the scales were merely level because, in the balance that contained the hope, he had thrown only four of the six words that make up the text. *"My grace is sufficient"*; he had no doubt about that, and it gave him encouragement. But *"for thee"*; he felt that, if only he could add those words to the others, it would turn the scales completely. "I had hope," he says, "yet because the *'for thee'* was left out, I was not contented, but prayed to God for *that* also. Wherefore, one day, when I was in a meeting of God's people, full of sadness and terror, these words did with great power suddenly break in upon me; *My grace is sufficient for thee, My grace is sufficient for thee, My grace is sufficient for thee*, three times together. And oh! methought that every word was a mighty word unto me; as *My* and *grace,* and *sufficient,* and *for thee;* they were then, and sometimes are still, far bigger than all others. Then, at last, that about Esau finding no place for repentance began to wax weak and withdraw and vanish, and this about the sufficiency of grace prevailed with peace and joy." And so the issue was reversed; the scale that held the hope over-weighed completely the scale that held the despair.

If it were not that others have passed through an identically similar experience, we should feel inclined to marvel at Bunyan's reluctance to cast into the balances the tail of the text: *My grace is sufficient — for thee!* It seems strange, I say, that Bunyan should have grasped with such confidence the *four* words and then boggled at the other *two.* And yet it is always easier to believe that there is a Savior for the world than to believe that there is a Savior *for me.* It is easy to believe that

> There is grace enough for thousands
> Of new worlds as great as this;
> There is room for fresh creations
> In that upper home of bliss;

but it is much harder to believe that there is grace and room *for me.*

Martin Luther believed implicitly and preached confidently that Christ died for all mankind, long before he could persuade himself that Christ died for Martin Luther. John Wesley crossed the Atlantic that he might proclaim the forgiveness of sins to the Indians; but it was not until he was verging upon middle life that he realized the possibility of the forgiveness of his own.

It is all very illogical, of course, and very absurd. If we can accept the *four* words, why not accept all *six?* If we credit the head of the text, why cavil at the tail? Sometimes the absurdity of such irrational behavior will break upon a man and set him laughing at his own stupidity.

Mr. Spurgeon had some such experience. "Gentlemen," he said, one Friday afternoon, in an address to his students, "Gentlemen, there are many passages of Scripture which you will never understand until some trying or singular experience shall inter-pret them to you. The other evening I was riding home after a heavy day's work; I was very wearied and sore depressed; and, swiftly and suddenly as a lightning flash, that text laid hold on me: *My grace is sufficient for thee!* On reaching home, I looked it up in the original, and at last it came to me in this way. MY *grace is sufficient for* THEE! 'Why,' I said to myself, 'I should think it is!' and I burst out laughing. I never fully understood what the holy laughter of Abraham was like until then. It seemed to make unbelief so absurd. It was as though some little fish, being very thirsty, was troubled about drinking the river dry; and Father Thames said: 'Drink away, little fish, my stream is sufficient for thee!' Or as if a little mouse in the granaries of Egypt, after seven years of plenty, feared lest it should die of famine, and Joseph said: 'Cheer up, little mouse, my granaries are sufficient for thee!'

"Again I imagined a man away up yonder on the mountain saying to himself: 'I fear I shall exhaust all the oxygen in the atmosphere.' But the earth cries: 'Breathe away, O man, and fill thy lungs; my atmosphere is sufficient for thee!' " John Bunyan enjoyed a moment's merriment of the same kind when he threw the last two words into the scale and saw his despair dwindle into insignificance on the instant.

III

Some such thought shines through the passage in which Paul tells us how the great words came to him. He was irritated by his thorn; he prayed repeatedly for its removal; but the only answer that he received was this: *My grace is sufficient for thee!* Grace sufficient for a thorn! It is an almost ludicrous association of ideas!

It is so easy for Bunyan to believe that the divine grace is sufficient for the wide, wide world; it is so difficult to realize that it is sufficient for him!

It is so easy for Wesley to believe in the forgiveness of sins; it is so difficult for him to believe in the forgiveness of his own!

It is so easy for Paul to believe in the grace that is sufficient to redeem a fallen race; it is so difficult for him to believe in the grace that can fortify him to endure his thorn!

And yet, in a fine essay on *Great Principles and Small Duties,* Dr. James Martineau has shown that it is the lowliest who most need the loftiest: it is the tiny thorn that calls for the most tremendous grace. The gravest mistake ever made by educationalists is, he says, the mistake of supposing that those who know little are good enough to teach those who know less. It is a tragedy, he declares, when the master is only one stage ahead of his pupil. "The ripest scholarship," he maintains, "is alone qualified to instruct the most complete ignorance." Mr. Martineau goes on to show that a soul occupied with great ideas best performs trivial duties. And, coming to the supreme example of his subject, he points out that "it was the peculiarity of the Savior's greatness, not that He stooped to the lowliest, but that, without stooping, He penetrated to the humblest wants. He not simply stepped aside to look at the most ignominious sorrows, but went directly to them, and lived wholly in them; scattered glorious miracles and sacred truths along the hidden by-paths and in the mean recesses of existence; serving the mendicant and the widow, blessing the child, healing the leprosy of body and of soul, and kneeling to wash even the traitor's feet." Here is a strange and marvelous and beautiful law! The loftiest for the lowliest! The greatest grace for the tiniest thorn!

Is it any wonder that, this being so, Paul felt that his splinter positively shone? *"I will glory in it,"* he cried, *"that the power of Christ may be billetted upon me."* He feels that his soul is like some rural hamlet into which a powerful regiment has marched. Every bed and barn is occupied by the soldiers. Who would not be irritated by a splinter, he asks, if the irritation leads to such an inrush of divine power and grace? It is like the pain of the oyster that is healed by a pearl.

And so, with Paul as with Bunyan, the grace turns the scales. It is better to have the pain if it brings the pearl. It is better to have a thorn in the one balance if it brings such grace into the opposite balance that one is better off *with* the thorn than *without* it.

Therein lies life's deepest secret — the secret that Catherine Booth and John Bunyan learned from the lips that unfolded it to Paul. In *The Master's Violin,* Myrtle Reed tells us the secret of the music that the old man's fingers wooed from the Cremona. You have but to look at the master, she says, and you will comprehend. "There he stands, a stately figure, grey and rugged, yet with a certain graciousness; simple, kindly, and yet austere; one who had accepted his sorrow, and, by some alchemy of the spirit, transmuted it into universal compassion, to speak, through the Cremona, to all who could understand!"

That is the secret — the old musician's secret; Catherine Booth's secret; Bunyan's secret; Paul's secret; the secret of all who have learned the text *by heart!*

My grace is sufficient for thee — the inrush of the grace turned Paul's torturing splinter into a cause for lifelong thankfulness!

My grace is sufficient for thee — the inrush of the grace turned

Mrs. Booth's fierce struggle into a ceaseless song!

My grace is sufficient for thee! To the man who, like John Bunyan, stands weighing his gladnesses and sadnesses with that text in his mind, it will seem that the one scale is overflowing and the other empty. For it is the glory of the grace that it takes what sadnesses there are and transmutes them into songs sublime.

16

JOHN G. PATON

(1824-1907)

John G. Paton was a Scottish Presbyterian missionary to the South Seas cannibals. His wife and infant son died shortly after arriving on the island of Tanna. He was forced to leave his station after four years, leaving behind all his possessions except his Bible and the few things that he could carry with him.

Paton traveled extensively in Australia, Great Britain, Canada, and the United States on behalf of the New Hebrides Mission; later returning to a neighboring island, Aniwa, he gave the people the New Testament and their first hymnbook in their own language.

Paton's son later resumed work among the savages of Tanna, and that island was won for Christ.

His text: "Lo, I am with you alway, even unto the end of the world" (Mathew 28:20).

I

I can see him now, as, stately and patriarchal, he walked up the desk room of the old college to address us. As that impressive and striking figure appeared at the door, every student instinctively sprang to his feet and remained standing till the Grand Old Man was seated. I thought that I had never seen a face more beautiful, a figure more picturesque. A visitant from another world could scarcely have proved more arresting or awe-inspiring. When it was announced that Dr. J. G. Paton, the veteran missionary to the New Hebrides, was coming to address the college, I expected to *hear* something thrilling and affecting; but, somehow, it did not occur to me that my *eyes* would be captivated as well. But, when the hero of my dreams appeared, a picture which I shall carry with me to my dying day was added to the gallery which my memory treasures.

This was in London many years ago. I little thought that afternoon that the apostolic form before me would one day sleep in an Australian grave, and that my own home would stand within half an hour's journey of his lovely resting-place.

In preparation for the task to which I now address myself, I paid a pilgrimage to the Boroondara Cemetery this afternoon, and read Dr. J. G. Paton's text bravely inscribed upon his tomb. It is not the kind of text that is usually engraved upon such monuments, but it is in every way appropriate to *him.* "In his private conversation," writes his son, the Rev. F. H. L. Paton, M.A., B.D., "in his private conversation and in his public addresses, my father was constantly quoting the words, *Lo, I am with you alway,* as the inspiration of his quietness and confidence in time of danger, and of his hope in the face of human impossibilities. So much was this realized by his family that we decided to inscribe that text upon his tomb in the Boroondara Cemetery. It seemed to all of us to sum up the essential elements in his faith, and the supreme source of his courage and endurance."

"Lo, I am with you alway!"
The secret of a quiet heart!
The secret of a gallant spirit!
The secret of a sunny faith!
The text so often on the tongue! The text upon the tomb!
"Lo, I am with you alway, even unto the end!"

II

The text is the tincture of miracle. Edna Lyall once wrote a novel — *We Two* — to show the wondrous magic that slumbers in those sacred syllables. *We Two* is the story of Erica Raeburn. Erica is the daughter of Luke Raeburn, the sceptic; and she has been taught from infancy to despise all holy things. But as life, with its stress and struggle, goes on, she finds that she cannot satisfy her soul with denials and negations. "At last," Edna Lyall says, "Erica's hopelessness, her sheer desperation, drove her to cry to the Possibly Existent." She stood at the open window of her little room, looking out into the summer night. Before she knew what had happened, she was praying!

"O God," she cried, "I have no reason to think that Thou art, except that there is such fearful need of Thee. I can see no single proof in all the world that Thou art here. But *if* Thou art, O Father, *if* Thou art, help me to know Thee! Show me what is true!"

A few days later the answer came. Erica was at the British Museum, making some extracts, in the ordinary course of her business, from the *Life of Livingstone.* All at once she came upon the extract from Livingstone's *Journal,* in which he speaks of his absolute reliance upon the text, *Lo, I am with you alway.* "It is the word," says Livingstone, "it is the word of a gentleman of the strictest and most sacred honor, and there's an end of it!" The words profoundly affected Erica. *Lo, I am with you alway!* They represented, not a Moral Principle, nor a Logical Proposition, but a Living Presence!

"Exactly how it came to her, Erica never knew, nor could she put in words the story of the next few minutes. When *God's great sunrise* finds us out, we have need of something higher than human speech: there *are* no words for it. All in a moment, the Christ who had been to her merely a noble character of ancient history became to her the most real and vital of all living realities. It was like coming into a new world; even dingy Bloomsbury seemed beautiful. Her face was so bright, so like the face of a happy child, that more than one passer-by was startled by it, lifted for a moment from sordid cares into a purer atmosphere."

All this is in the early part of the book; but even in the last chapter Erica is still rejoicing in her text, and in the deathless treasure which it so suddenly unfolded to her. *God's great sunrise* had come to stay.

III

God's great sunrise broke upon J. G. Paton amid the sanctities and simplicities of his Scottish home. He was only a boy when he learned the sublime secret to which the text gives expression, and it was his father who revealed it to him. In a passage that has taken its place among our spiritual classics, he has described the little Dumfriesshire cottage, with its "but" and its "ben," and the tiny apartment in which he used to hear his father at prayer. And whenever the good man issued from that cottage sanctuary, there was a light in his face which, Dr. Paton says, the outside world could never understand; "but we children knew that it was *a reflection of the Divine Presence in which his life was lived."*

And, continuing this touching story, Dr. Paton describes the impression that his father's prayers in that little room made upon his boyish mind. "Never," he says, "in temple or cathedral, on mountain or in glen, can I hope to feel that the Lord God is more near, more visibly walking and talking with men, than under that humble cottage roof of thatch and oaken wattles. Though everything else in religion were by some unthinkable catastrophe to be swept out of memory, my soul would wander back to those early scenes, and would shut itself up once again in that sanctuary closet, and, hearing still the echoes of those cries to God, would hurl back all doubt with the victorious appeal: *He walked with God; why may not I?"*

Why, indeed? J. G. Paton resolved that his father's religion should be *his* religion; his father's God *his* God. He pinned his faith to the sublime assurance on which his father rested with such serenity. During all his adventurous years in the South Seas, he relied implicitly upon it, and, as a result, he says that he felt immortal till his work was done. "Trials and hairbreadth escapes only strengthened my faith and nerved me for more to follow; and they trod swiftly enough upon each other's heels. Without that abiding consciousness of the presence and power of my Lord and Savior, nothing in the world could have preserved me from losing my reason and perishing miserably. His words *Lo, I am with you alway, even unto the end* became to me so real that it would not have startled me to behold Him, as Stephen did, gazing down upon the scene. It is the sober truth that I had my nearest and most intimate glimpses of the presence of my Lord in those dread moments when musket, club, or spear was being levelled at my life."

Thus, then, J. G. Paton, as a boy in his Scottish home, learned the unutterable value of the text, *Lo, I am with you alway.* Thus, too, twenty years later, he went out to his life-work, singing in his soul those golden words.

IV

He very quickly tested their efficacy and power. It was on the fifth of November, 1858, that the young Scotsman and his wife first landed on Tanna. It was purely a cannibal island in those days, and the white man found his faith in his text severely tried.

"My first impressions," he tells us, "drove me to the verge of utter dismay. On beholding the natives in their paint and nakedness and misery, my heart was as full of horror as of pity. Had I given up my much-beloved work, and my dear people in Glasgow, with so many delightful associations, to consecrate my life to these degraded creatures? Was it possible to teach them right and wrong, to Christianize, or even to civilize them?" But this, he goes on to say, was only a passing feeling. He soon reminded himself that he and his wife were not undertaking the work at their own charges. They were not alone. The transformation of the natives seemed impossible; but his son had already told us that the text often braced him to face the apparently impossible. It did then.

If ever a man seemed lonely, J. G. Paton seemed lonely when, three months later, he had to dig with his own hands a grave for his young wife and his baby boy. In spite of all pleas and remonstrances, Mrs. Paton had insisted on accompanying him, and now, the only white man on the island, he was compelled to lay her to rest on this savage spot. "Let those," he says, "who have ever passed through similar darkness — darkness as of midnight — feel for me; as for all others, it would be more than vain to try to paint my sorrows. I was stunned: my reason seemed almost to give way: I built a wall of coral round the grave, and covered the top with beautiful white coral, broken small as gravel; and that spot became my sacred and much-frequented shrine during all the years that, amidst difficulties, dangers, and deaths, I labored for the salvation of these savage islanders. Whenever Tanna turns to the Lord and is won for Christ, men will find the memory of that spot still green. It was there that I claimed for God the land in which I had buried my dead with faith and hope."

With faith and hope! What faith? What hope? It was the faith and the hope of his text! *Lo, I am with you alway!* "I was never altogether forsaken," he says, in his story of that dreadful time. "The ever-merciful Lord sustained me to lay the precious dust of my loved ones in the same quiet grave. But for Jesus, and the fellowship He vouchsafed me there, I must have gone mad and died beside that lonely grave!"

A few weeks afterwards, George Augustus Selwyn, the pioneer Bishop of New Zealand, and James Coleridge Patteson, the martyr Bishop of Melanesia, chanced to call at the island. They had met Mrs. Paton — then the picture of perfect health — a few months previously, and were shocked beyond measure to learn the story of the missionary's sorrow. "Standing with me beside the grave of mother and child," says Dr. Paton, "I weeping aloud on his right hand, and Patteson sobbing silently on his left, the good Bishop Selwyn poured out his heart to God amidst sobs and tears, during which he laid his hands on my head and invoked heaven's richest consolations and blessings on me and my trying labors. The virtue of that kind of episcopal consecration I did, and do, most warmly appreciate." To the end of his days, Dr. Selwyn used to speak of Dr. Paton as one of the bravest and one of the saintliest men he had ever met.

It was thus, at the very outset of his illustrious career, that Dr. Paton discovered the divine dependability of his text.

"Lo, I am with you alway!"

"I was never altogether forsaken!"

"The ever-merciful Lord sustained me!"

"But for Jesus, I must have gone mad and died!"

"Lo, I am with you alway, even unto the end!"

In his extremity, J. G. Paton threw himself upon the promise; and the promise held.

V

Through the eventful years that followed, the text was his constant companion. He faces death in a hundred forms, but the episode invariably closes with some such record as this:

"During the crisis, I felt generally calm and firm of soul, standing erect and with my whole weight on the promise, *Lo, I am with you alway*. Precious promise! How often I adore Jesus for it and rejoice in it! Blessed be His name!" or this:

"I have always felt that His promise, *Lo, I am with you alway*, is a reality, and that He is with His servants to support and bless them even unto the end of the world."

From many such instances, I cull one as typical of the rest.

In 1862 the whole island was convulsed by tribal warfare. In their frenzy the natives threatened to destroy both the mission station and the missionary. Nowar, a friendly chief, urged Dr. Paton to fly into the bush and hide in a large chestnut tree there. "Climb up into it," he said, "and remain till the moon rises." He did so, and, concealed in that leafy shelter, saw the blacks beating the bushes around in their eager search for himself.

"The hours that I spent in that chestnut tree," writes Dr. Paton, "still live before me. I heard the frequent discharge of muskets and the hideous yells of the savages. Yet never, in all my sorrows, did my Lord draw nearer to me. I was alone, yet not alone. I would cheerfully spend many nights alone in such a tree to feel again my Savior's spiritual presence as I felt it that night."

About midnight a messenger came to advise him to go down to the beach. "Pleading for my Lord's continued presence, I could but obey. My life now hung on a very slender thread. But my comfort and joy sprang from the words *Lo, I am with you alway.* Pleading this promise, I followed my guide."

The crisis passed. "I confess," Dr. Paton says, "that I often felt my brain reeling, my sight coming and going, and my knees smiting together when thus brought face to face with a violent death. Still, I was never left without hearing that promise coming up through the darkness and the anguish in all its consoling and supporting power: *Lo, I am with you alway."*

Some years later, Dr. Paton married again, and settled at Aniwa. But, on a notable occasion, he revisited Tanna. Old Nowar was delighted, and begged them to remain.

"We have plenty of food," he assured Mrs. Paton. "While I have a yam or a banana, you shall not want." Mrs. Paton said that she was sure of it.

"We are many!" he cried, pointing to his warriors; "we are strong; we can always protect you!"

"I am not afraid," she smilingly replied.

"Then," says Dr. Paton, "he led us to that chestnut tree in the branches of which I had sheltered during that lonely and memorable night when all hope of earthly deliverance had perished, and said to Mrs. Paton, with a manifest touch of genuine emotion, 'The God who protected Missi in the tree will always protect you!'"

The Form in the Furnace — the Form that was like unto the Son of God — was seen by Nebuchadnezzar as well as by the Three Hebrew Children. And the Presence of Him who had said *Lo, I am with you alway* was recognized by the barbarians of Tanna, as well as by Dr. Paton himself. Their sharp eyes soon detected that the white man was never left to his own resources.

VI

Dr. Paton lived to be eighty-three, and his promise never failed him. Even when he was weakest, Mr. Langridge says, his heart never doubted for a moment, and, whenever any one came to see him, he rejoiced to tell them how unclouded was the peace within, and how intensely real and sustaining he found the promises of God's Word. He used often to say, "With me there is not a shadow or a cloud: all is perfect peace and joy in believing." A moment after his last breath had been drawn, the lines of pain were smoothed from his fine face, as by an invisible hand. He had actually gazed upon the Savior, whose vivid presence had been the radiant reality of his life. *God's great sunrise* had broken upon him with even richer splendor; and, as the clouds reflect the afterglow of sunset, so his pale face reflected the afterglow of that beatific vision. He was laid to rest next day in the grave that I visited this afternoon; and now every pilgrim to his sepulchre sees his text boldly inscribed upon his tomb.

17

JAMES HUDSON TAYLOR
(1832-1905)

J. Hudson Taylor was the founder of the China Inland Mission (Overseas Missionary Fellowship). His interest in China went back to his childhood when he often told his friends that he was going there. This interest grew after his conversion to Christ. In fact, it became his constant thought when he realized that the country had "360 million souls, without God or hope" and "more than twelve millions of our fellow creatures dying every year without any of the consolations of the Gospel."

Taylor put God first in his life. He read the Bible through forty times in forty years. He got up at 5:00 in the morning to spend time with God. He adopted the policy of prayer and faith for the support of the mission.

At the time of his death the mission had 849 missionaries on 205 stations and 125,000 Chinese Christians.

His text: "When Jesus therefore had received the vinegar, he said, It is finished: and he bowed his head, and gave up the ghost" (John 19:30).

I

The day on which James Hudson Taylor — then a boy in his teens — found himself confronted by that tremendous text was, as he himself testified in old age, "a day that he could never forget." It is a day that China can never forget; a day that the world can never forget. It was a holiday; everybody was away from home; and the boy found time hanging heavily upon his hands. In an aimless way he wandered, during the afternoon, into his father's library, and poked about among the shelves. "I tried," he says, "to find some book with which to while away the leaden hours. Nothing attracting me, I turned over a basket of pamphlets and selected from among them a tract that looked interesting. I knew that it would have a story at the beginning and a moral at the close; but I promised myself that I would enjoy the story and leave the rest. It would be easy to put away the tract as soon as it should seem prosy."

He scampers off to the stable-loft, throws himself on the hay, and plunges into the book. He is captivated by the narrative, and finds it impossible to drop the book when the story comes to an end. He reads on and on. He is rewarded by one great golden word whose significance he has never before discovered: *"The Finished Work of Christ!"* The theme entrances him; and at last he only rises from his bed in the soft hay that he might kneel on the hard floor of the loft and surrender his young life to the Savior who had surrendered everything for him. If, he asked himself, as he lay upon the hay, if the whole work was finished, and the whole debt paid upon the Cross, what is there left for me to do? "And then," he tells us, "there dawned upon me the joyous conviction that there was nothing in the world to be done but to fall upon my knees, accept the Savior and praise Him for evermore."

"It is finished!"

"When Jesus therefore had received the vinegar, he said, 'It is finished!' and He bowed His head and gave up the ghost."

"Then there dawned upon me the joyous conviction that, since the whole work was finished and the whole debt paid upon the Cross, there was nothing for me to do but to fall upon my knees, accept the Savior and praise Him for evermore!"

II

"It is finished!"

It is really only one word: the greatest word ever uttered; we must examine it for a moment as a lapidary examines under a powerful glass a rare and costly gem.

It was a *farmer's* word. When, into his herd, there was born an animal so beautiful and shapely that it seemed absolutely destitute of faults and defects, the farmer gazed upon the creature with proud, delighted eyes. *"Tetelestai!"* he said, *"tetelestai!"*

It was an *artist's* word. When the painter or the sculptor had put the last finishing touches to the vivid landscape or the marble bust, he would stand back a few feet to admire his masterpiece, and, seeing in it nothing that called for correction or improvement, would murmur fondly, *"Tetelestai! tetelestai!"*

It was a *priestly* word. When some devout worshiper, overflowing with gratitude for mercies shown him, brought to the temple a lamb without spot or blemish, the pride of the whole flock, the priest, more accustomed to seeing the blind and defective animals led to the altar, would look admiringly upon the pretty creature. *"Tetelestai!"* he would say, *"tetelestai!"*

And when, in the fullness of time, the Lamb of God offered Himself on the altar of the ages, He rejoiced with a joy so triumphant that it bore down all His anguish before it. The sacrifice was stainless, perfect, finished! *"He cried with a loud voice* Tetelestai! *and gave up the ghost."*

This divine self-satisfaction appears only twice, once in each Testament. When He completed the work of Creation, He looked upon it and said that it was very good; when He completed the work of Redemption He cried with a loud voice *Tetelestai!* It means exactly the same thing.

III

The joy of finishing and of finishing well! How passionately good men have coveted for themselves that ecstasy! I think of those pathetic entries in Livingstone's journal. "Oh, to finish my work!" he writes again and again. He is haunted by the vision of the unseen waters, the fountains of the Nile. Will he live to discover them? "Oh, to finish!" he cries; "if only I could finish my work!"

I think of Henry Buckle, the author of the *History of Civilization*. He is overtaken by fever at Nazareth and dies at Damascus. In his delirium he raves continually about his book, his still unfinished book. "Oh, to finish my book!" And with the words, "My book! my book!" upon his burning lips, his spirit slips away.

I think of Henry Martyn sitting amidst the delicious and fragrant shades of a Persian garden, weeping at having to leave the work that he seemed to have only just begun. I think of Doré taking a sad farewell of his unfinished *Vale of Tears;* of Dickens tearing himself from the manuscript that he knew would never be completed; of Macaulay looking with wistful and longing eyes at the *History* and *The Armada* that must for ever stand as "fragments"; and a host besides. Life is often represented by a broken column in the churchyard. Men long, but long in vain, for the priceless privilege of finishing their work.

IV

The joy of finishing and of finishing well! There is no joy on earth comparable to this. Who is there that has not read a dozen times the immortal postscript that Gibbons added to his *Decline and Fall?* He describes the tumult of emotion with which, after twenty years of closest application, he wrote the last line of the last chapter of the last volume of his masterpiece. It was a glorious summer's night at Lausanne. "After laying down my pen," he says, "I took several turns in a covered walk of acacias which commands a prospect of the country, the lake and the mountains. The air was temperate, the sky was serene, the silver orb of the moon was reflected from the waters, and all nature was silent." It was the greatest moment of his life. We recall, too, the similar experience of Sir Archibald Alison. "As I approached the closing sentence of my *History of the Empire,*" he says, "I went up to Mrs. Alison to call her down to witness the conclusion, and she saw the last words of the work written, and signed her name on the margin. It would be affectation to conceal the deep emotion that I felt at this event."

Or think of the last hours of the Venerable Bede. Living away back in the early dawn of our English story — twelve centuries ago — the old man had set himself to translate the Gospel of John into our native speech. Cuthbert, one of his young disciples, has bequeathed to us the touching record. As the work approached completion, he says, death drew on apace. The aged scholar was racked with pain; sleep forsook him; he could scarcely breathe. The young man who wrote at his dictation implored him to desist. But he would not rest. They came at length to the final chapter; could he possibly live till it was done?

"And now, dear master," exclaimed the young scribe tremblingly, "only one sentence remains!" He read the words and the sinking man feebly recited the English equivalents.

"It is finished, dear master!" cried the youth excitedly.

"Ay, *it is finished!*" echoed the dying saint; "lift me up, place me at that window of my cell at which I have so often prayed to God. Now glory be to the Father and to the Son and to the Holy

Ghost!" And, with these triumphant words, the beautiful spirit passed to its rest and its reward.

V

In his own narrative of his conversion, Hudson Taylor quotes James Proctor's well-known hymn — the hymn that Froude criticizes so severely:

> Nothing either great or small,
> Nothing, sinner, no;
> Jesus did it, did it all,
> Long, long ago.
>
> *"It is Finished!"* yes, indeed,
> Finished every jot;
> Sinner, this is all you need;
> Tell me, is it not?
>
> Cast your deadly doing down,
> Down at Jesus' feet;
> Stand in Him, in Him alone,
> Gloriously complete.

Froude maintains that these verses are immoral. It is only by "doing," he argues, that the work of the world can ever get done. And if you describe "doing" as "deadly" you set a premium upon indolence and lessen the probabilities of attainment. The best answer to Froude's plausible contention is the *Life of Hudson Taylor*. Hudson Taylor became convinced, as a boy, that "the whole work was finished and the whole debt paid." "There is nothing for me to do," he says, "but to fall down on my knees and accept the Savior." The chapter in his biography that tells of this spiritual crisis is entitled "The Finished Work of Christ," and it is headed by the quotation:

> Upon a life I did not live,
> Upon a death I did not die,
> Another's life, Another's death,
> I stake my whole eternity.

And, as I have said, the very words that Froude so bitterly condemns are quoted by Hudson Taylor as a reflection of his own experience. And the result? The result is that Hudson Taylor became one of the most prodigious toilers of all time. So far from his trust in "the Finished Work of Christ" inclining him to indolence, he felt that he must toil most terribly to make so perfect a Savior known to the whole wide world.

There lies on my desk a Birthday Book which I very highly value. It was given me at the docks by Mr. Thomas Spurgeon as I was leaving England. If you open it at the twenty-first of May you will find these words: " *'Simply to Thy Cross I cling' is but half of the Gospel. No one is really clinging to the Cross who is not at the same time faithfully following Christ and doing whatsoever He commands";* and against those words of Dr. J. R. Miller's in my Birthday Book, you may see the autograph of *J. Hudson Taylor.* He was our guest at the Mosgiel Manse when he set his signature to those striking and significant sentences.

VI

"We Build Like Giants; we Finish Like Jewellers!" — so the old Egyptians wrote over the portals of their palaces and temples. I like to think that the most gigantic task ever attempted on this planet — the work of the world's redemption — was finished with a precision and a nicety that no jeweller could rival.

"It is finished!" He cried from the Cross.

"Tetelestai! Tetelestai!"

When He looked upon His work in Creation and saw that it was good, He placed it beyond the power of man to improve upon it.

> To gild refined gold, to paint the lily,
> To throw a perfume on the violet,
> To smooth the ice, or add another hue
> Unto the rainbow, or with taper-light
> To seek the beauteous eye of heaven to garnish,
> Is wasteful and ridiculous excess.

And, similarly, when He looked upon His work in Redemption and cried triumphantly "Tetelestai," He placed it beyond the power of any man to add to it.

There are times when any addition is a subtraction. Some years ago, the White House at Washington — the residence of the American Presidents — was in the hands of the painters and decorators. Two large entrance doors had been painted to represent black walnut. The contractor ordered his men to scrape and clean them in readiness for repainting, and they set to work. But when their knives penetrated to the solid timber, they discovered to their astonishment that it was heavy mahogany of a most exquisite natural grain! The work of that earlier decorator, so far from adding to the beauty of the timber, had only served to conceal its essential and inherent glory. It is easy enough to add to the wonders of Creation or of Redemption; but you can never add without subtracting. *"It is finished!"*

VII

Many years ago, Ebenezer Wooton, an earnest but eccentric evangelist, was conducting a series of summer evening services on the village green at Lidford Brook. The last meeting had been held; the crowd was melting slowly away; and the evangelist was engaged in taking down the marquee. All at once a young fellow approached him and asked, casually rather than earnestly, "Mr. Wooton, what must I do to be saved?" The preacher took the measure of his man.

"Too late!" he said, in a matter-of-fact kind of way, glancing up from a somewhat obstinate tent-peg with which he was struggling. "Too late, my friend, too late!" The young fellow was startled.

"Oh, don't say that, Mr. Wooton!" he pleaded, a new note coming into his voice. "Surely it isn't too late just because the meetings are over?"

"Yes, my friend," exclaimed the evangelist, dropping the cord in his hand, straightening himself up, and looking right into the face of his questioner, "it's too late! You want to know what you must *do* to be saved, and I tell you that you're hundreds of years too late! The work of salvation is done, completed, *finished!* It was finished on the Cross; Jesus said so with the last breath that He drew! What more do you want?"

And, then and there, it dawned upon the now earnest inquirer on the village green as, at about the same time, it dawned upon young Hudson Taylor in the hay-loft, that *"since the whole work was finished and the whole debt paid upon the Cross, there was nothing for him to do but to fall upon his knees and accept the Savior."* And, there, under the elms, the sentinel stars witnessing the great transaction, he kneeled in glad thanksgiving and rested his soul for time and for eternity on *"the Finished Work of Christ."*

VIII

"The Finished Work of Christ!"
"Tetelestai! Tetelestai!"
"It is finished!"

It is not a sigh of relief at having reached the end of things. It is the unutterable joy of the artist who, putting the last touches to the picture that has engrossed him for so long, sees in it the realization of all his dreams and can nowhere find room for improvement. Only once in the world's history did a finishing touch bring a work to absolute perfection; and on that day of days a single flaw would have shattered the hope of the ages.

18

CHARLES SPURGEON
(1834-1892)

Charles Spurgeon, converted at age fifteen, preached his first sermon a year later. By the time he was twenty-two, he was the most popular preacher of his day, often preaching to audiences numbering 10,000.

Metropolitan Tabernacle in London, seating 6,000 people, was built in 1861 to accommodate the large crowds. Spurgeon ministered at this tabernacle until his death.

He began publishing his weekly sermons in 1855. More than 2,000 sermons were published in his lifetime and eventually compiled into a forty-nine-volume set entitled *The Metropolitan Pulpit.*

Spurgeon also founded a Pastors' College. Ministers from that college were sent throughout Great Britain and also to Australia, New Zealand, Canada, Haiti, the Falkland Islands, South America, South Africa, and Holland.

He established an orphanage accommodating 500 children. A monthly church publication, *The Sword and the Trowel,* began in 1865 and continued for twenty-eight years.

During his lifetime Spurgeon wrote one hundred thirty-five volumes and edited another twenty-eight.

While known as a Baptist preacher, Spurgeon was also a bookman. "He knew books, he wrote books, he read books, he distributed books, he received books."

His text: "Look unto me, and be ye saved, all the ends of the earth" (Isaiah 45:22).

I

Snow! Snow! Snow!

It was the first Sunday of the New Year, and this was how it opened! On roads and footpaths the snow was already many inches deep; the fields were a sheet of blinding whiteness, and the flakes were still falling as though they never meant to stop. As the caretaker fought his way through the storm from his cottage to the chapel in Artillery Street, he wondered whether, on such a wild and wintry day, any one would venture out. It would be strange if, on the very first Sunday morning of the year, there should be no service. He unbolted the chapel doors and lit the furnace under the stove.

Half an hour later, two men were seen bravely trudging their way through the snow-drifts; and, as they stood on the chapel steps, their faces flushed with their recent exertions, they laughingly shook the snow from off their hats and overcoats. What a morning, to be sure!

By eleven o'clock about a dozen others had arrived; but where was the minister? They waited; but he did not come. He lived at a distance, and, in all probability, had found the roads impassable. What was to be done? The stewards looked at each other and surveyed the congregation. Except for a boy of fifteen sitting under the gallery, every face was known to them, and the range of selection was not great.

There were whisperings and hasty consultations, and at last one of the two men who were first to arrive — "a poor, thin-looking man, a shoemaker, a tailor, or something of that sort" —yielded to the murmured entreaties of the others and mounted the pulpit steps. He glanced nervously round upon nearly three hundred empty seats. Nearly, but not quite! For there were a dozen or fifteen of the regular worshippers present, and there was the boy sitting under the gallery. People who had braved such a morning deserved all the help that he could give them, and the strange boy under the gallery ought not to be sent back into the storm feeling that there was nothing in the service for him. And so the preacher determined to make the most of the opportunity; and he did.

The boy sitting under the gallery! A marble tablet now adorns the wall near the seat which he occupied that snowy day. The inscription records that, that very morning, the boy sitting under the gallery was converted! He was only fifteen and he died at fifty-seven. But, in the course of the intervening years, he preached the gospel to millions and led thousands and thousands into the kingdom and service of Jesus Christ.

"Let preachers study this story!" says Sir William Robertson Nicoll. "Let them believe that, under the most adverse circumstances, they may do a work that will tell on the universe for ever. It was a great thing to have converted Charles Haddon Spurgeon; and who knows but he may have in the smallest and humblest congregation in the world some lad as well worth converting as was he?"

II

Snow! Snow! Snow!

The boy sitting under the gallery had purposed attending quite another place of worship that Sunday morning. No thought of the little chapel in Artillery Street occurred to him as he strode out into the storm. Not that he was very particular. Ever since he was ten years of age he had felt restless and ill at ease whenever his mind turned to the things that are unseen and eternal. "I had been about five years in the most fearful distress of mind," he says. "I thought the sun was blotted out of my sky, that I had so sinned against God that there was no hope for me!" He prayed, but never had a glimpse of an answer. He attended every place of worship in the town; but no man had a message for a youth who only wanted to know what he must do to be saved.

With the first Sunday of the New Year he purposed trying yet another of these ecclesiastical experiments. But in making his plans he had not reckoned on the ferocity of the storm. "I sometimes think," he said, years afterwards, "I sometimes think I might have been in darkness and despair now, had it not been for the goodness of God in sending a snowstorm on Sunday morning, January 6, 1850, when I was going to a place of worship. When I could go no further I turned down a court and came to a little Primitive Methodist chapel."

Thus the strange boy sitting under the gallery came to be seen by the impromptu speaker that snowy morning! Thus, as so often happens, a broken program pointed the path of destiny! Who says that two wrongs can never make a right? Let them look at this! The plans at the chapel went wrong: the minister was snowed up. The plans of the boy under the gallery went wrong: the snowstorm shut him off from the church of his choice. Those two wrongs together made one tremendous right; for out of those shattered plans and programs came an event that has incalculably enriched mankind.

III

Snow! Snow! Snow!

And the very snow seemed to mock his misery. It taunted him as he walked to church that morning. Each virgin snowflake as it fluttered before his face and fell at his feet only emphasized the dreadful pollution within. "My original and inward pollution!" he cries with Bunyan; "I was more loathsome in mine own eyes than a toad. Sin and corruption would as naturally bubble out of my heart as water out of a fountain. I thought that every one had a better heart than I had. At the sight of my own vileness I fell deeply into despair." These words of Bunyan's exactly reflect, he tells us, his own secret and spiritual history. And the white, white snow only intensified the agonizing consciousness of defilement.

In the expressive phraseology of the Church of England Communion Service, "the remembrance of his sins was grievous unto him; the burden of them was intolerable." "I counted the estate of everything that God had made far better than this dreadful state of mind was: yea, gladly would I have been in the condition of a dog or a horse; for I knew they had no souls to perish under the weight of sin as mine was like to do."

"Many and many a time," says Mr. Thomas Spurgeon, "my father told me that, in those early days, he was so stormtossed and distressed by reason of his sins that he found himself envying the very beasts in the field and the toads by the wayside!" So stormtossed! The storm that raged around him that January morning was in perfect keeping with the storm within; but oh, for the whiteness, the pure, unsullied whiteness, of the falling snow!

IV

Snow! Snow! Snow!

From out of that taunting panorama of purity the boy passed into the cavernous gloom of the almost empty building. Its leaden heaviness matched the mood of his spirit, and he stole furtively to a seat under the gallery. He noticed the long pause; the anxious glances which the stewards exchanged with each other; and, a little later, the whispered consultations. He watched curiously as the hastily-appointed preacher — "a shoemaker or something of that sort" — awkwardly ascended the pulpit. "The man was," Mr. Spurgeon tells us, "really stupid, as you would say. He was obliged to stick to his text for the simple reason that he had nothing else to say. His text was, *'Look unto Me and be ye saved, all the ends of the earth.'*

"He did not even pronounce the words rightly, but that did not matter. There was, I thought, a glimpse of hope for me in the text, and I listened as though my life depended upon what I heard. In about ten minutes the preacher had got to the end of his tether. Then he saw me sitting under the gallery; and I daresay, with so few present, he knew me to be a stranger. He then said: 'Young man, you look very miserable.'

"Well, I did; but I had not been accustomed to have remarks made from the pulpit on my personal appearance. However, it was a good blow, well struck.

"He continued: 'And you will always be miserable — miserable in life, and miserable in death — if you do not obey my text. But if you obey now, this moment, you will be saved!' Then he shouted, as only a Primitive Methodist can shout, 'Young man, look to Jesus! look, look, *look!*' I did; and, then and there, the cloud was gone, the darkness had rolled away, and that moment I saw the sun! I could have risen on the instant and sung with the most enthusiastic of them of the precious blood of Christ and of the simple faith which looks alone to Him. Oh, that somebody had told me before! In their own earnest way, they sang a Hallelujah before they went home, and I joined in it!"

The snow around!
The defilement within!
"Look unto Me and be ye saved, all the ends of the earth!"
"Precious blood . . . and simple faith!"
"I sang a Hallelujah!"

V

Snow! Snow! Snow!

The snow was falling as fast as ever when the boy sitting under the gallery rose and left the building. The storm raged just as fiercely. And yet the snow was not the same snow! Everything was changed. Mr. Moody has told us that, on the day of his conversion, all the birds in the hedgerow seemed to be singing newer and blither songs. Dr. Campbell Morgan declares that the very leaves on the trees appeared to him more beautiful on the day that witnessed the greatest spiritual crisis in his career. Frank Bullen was led to Christ in a little New Zealand port which I have often visited, by a worker whom I knew well. And he used to say that, next morning, he climbed the summit of a mountain nearby and the whole landscape seemed changed. Everything had been transformed in the night!

> Heaven above is softer blue,
> Earth around a deeper green,
> Something lives in every hue
> Christless eyes have never seen.
>
> Birds with gladder songs o'erflow,
> Flowers with richer beauties shine,
> Since I knew, as now I know,
> I am His and He is mine!

"I was now so taken with the love of God," says Bunyan — and here again Mr. Spurgeon says that the words might have been his own — "I was now so taken with the love and mercy of God that I could not tell how to contain till I got home. I thought I could have spoken of His love, and told of His mercy, even to the very crows that sat upon the ploughed lands before me, had they been capable of understanding me."

As the boy from under the gallery walked home that morning he laughed at the storm, and the snow that had mocked him coming sang to him as he returned. "The snow was lying deep," he says, "and more was falling. But those words of David kept ringing through my heart, *'Wash me, and I shall be whiter than snow!'* It seemed to me as if all Nature was in accord with the blessed deliverance from sin which I had found in a moment by looking to Jesus Christ!"

The mockery of the snow!
The text amidst the snow!
The music of the snow!
Whiter than the snow!
"Look unto Me and be ye saved!"
"Wash me, and I shall be whiter than snow!"

VI

"Look unto Me and be ye saved!"

Look! Look! Look!

I look to my doctor to heal me when I am hurt; I look to my lawyer to advise me when I am perplexed; I look to my tradesmen to bring my daily supplies to my door; but there is only One to whom I can look when my soul cries out for deliverance.

"Look unto Me and be ye saved, all the ends of the earth!"

"Look! Look! Look!" cried the preacher.

"I looked," says Mr. Spurgeon, "until I could almost have looked my eyes away; and in heaven I will look still, in joy unutterable!"

Happy the preacher, however unlettered, who, knowing little else, knows how to direct such wistful and hungry eyes to the only possible fountain of satisfaction!

19

JAMES CHALMERS
(1841-1901)

When James Chalmers was fifteen years old, he vowed to take the gospel to the cannibals. He was not converted until the age of eighteen and, after hearing of the power of the gospel over the cannibals in the South Sea Islands, applied to the London Missionary Society. In 1866 Chalmers and his new bride left for the Cook Islands of Polynesia, arriving in 1867.

For the next ten years Chalmers carried on the work begun by John Williams, the "Apostle of Polynesia," but he longed for the unevangelized areas, especially New Guinea. He opened up a wide area through exploration and saw entire tribes transformed by the gospel. He won the hearts of the people through faith, prayer, kindness, firmness, and heroism. A training school was established in Port Moresby.

In April 1901, Chalmers, along with missionary colleague Oliver Tomkins and twelve native Christians, was massacred, beheaded, and eaten by cannibals in an area not visited before.

A statue of Chalmers and a chapel have been built in Port Moresby, Papua, New Guinea, in his honor. His ministry and influence are felt throughout the South Sea Islands even today.

His text: "And the Spirit and the Bride say, Come. And let him that heareth say, Come. And let him that is athirst come. And whosoever will, let him take the water of life freely" (Revelation 22:17).

I

He was a "broth of a boy," his biographer tells us. He lived chiefly on boots and boxes. Eager to know what lay beyond the ranges, he wore out more boots than his poor parents found it easy to provide. Taunted by the constant vision of the restless waters, he put out to sea in broken boxes and leaky barrels, that he might follow in the wake of the great navigators.

He was a born adventurer. Almost as soon as he first opened his eyes and looked around him, he felt that the world was very wide and vowed that he would find its utmost edges. From his explorations of the hills and glens around his village home, he often returned too exhausted either to eat or sleep. From his ventures upon the ocean he was more than once brought home on a plank, apparently drowned. "The wind and the sea were his playmates," we are told; "he was as much at home in the water as on the land; in fishing, sailing, climbing over the rocks, and wandering among the silent hills, he spent a free, careless, happy boyhood." Every day had its own romance, its hairbreadth escape, its thrilling adventure.

Therein lies the difference between a man and a beast. At just about the time at which James Chalmers was born in Scotland, Captain Sturt led his famous expedition into the hot and dusty heart of Australia. When he reached Cooper's Creek on the return journey, he found that he had more horses than he would be able to feed, so he turned one of them out on the banks of the creek and left it there. When Burke and Wills reached Cooper's Creek twenty years later, the horse was still grazing peacefully on the side of the stream, and looked up at the explorers with no more surprise or excitement than it would have shown if but twenty hours had passed since it last saw human faces. It had found air to breathe and water to drink and grass to nibble; what did it care about the world?

But with man it is otherwise. He wants to know what is on the other side of the hill, what is on the other side of the water, what is on the other side of the world! If he cannot go North, South, East and West himself, he must at least have his newspaper; and the newspaper brings all the ends of the earth every morning to his doorstep and his breakfast table. This, I say, is the difference between a beast and a man; and James Chalmers — known in New Guinea as the most magnificent specimen of humanity on the islands — was every inch *a man*.

II

But his text? What was James Chalmers' text? When he was eighteen years of age, Scotland found herself in the throes of a great religious revival. In the sweep of this historic movement, a couple of evangelists from the North of Ireland announce that they will conduct a series of evangelistic meetings at Inverary. But Chalmers and a band of daring young spirits under his leadership feel that this is an innovation which they must strenuously resist. They agree to break up the meetings.

A friend, however, with much difficulty persuades Chalmers to attend the first meeting and judge for himself whether or not his project is a worthy one. "It was raining hard," he says, in some autobiographical notes found among his treasures after the massacre, "it was raining hard, but I started; and on arriving at the bottom of the stairs I listened while they sang 'All people that on earth do dwell' to the tune 'Old Hundred,' and I thought I had never heard such singing before — so solemn, yet so joyful. I ascended the steps and entered. There was a large congregation and all intensely in earnest. The younger of the evangelists was the first to speak. He announced as his text the words: *'The Spirit and the Bride say, Come; and let him that heareth say, Come; and let him that is athirst come; and whosoever will, let him take the water of life freely.'* He spoke directly to me. I felt it much; but at the close I hurried away back to town. I returned the Bible to the friend who, having persuaded me to go, had lent it to me, but I was too upset to speak much to him."

On the following Sunday night, he was, he says, "pierced through and through, and felt lost beyond all hope of salvation." On the Monday, the local minister, the Rev. Gilbert Meikle, who had exercised a deep influence over his early childhood, came to see him and assured him that the blood of Jesus Christ, God's Son, could cleanse him from all sin. This timely visit convinced him that deliverance was at any rate possible. Gradually he came to feel that the voices to which he was listening were, in reality, the Voice of God. "Then," he says, "I believed unto salvation."

"He felt that the voices to which he was listening were, in reality, the Voice of God." That is precisely what the text says. *"The Spirit and the Bride say, Come."* The Bride only says *"Come"* because the Spirit says *"Come";* the Church only says *"Come"* because her Lord says *"Come";* the evangelists only said *"Come"* because the Voice Divine says *"Come.""He* felt that the voices to

which he was listening were, in reality, the Voice of God, and he believed unto salvation."

The Spirit said, Come!
The Bride said, Come!
Let him that is athirst come!
"*I was athirst,*" says Chalmers, "*and I came!*"

And thus a great text began, in a great soul, the manufacture of a great history.

III

Forty years later a thrill of horror electrified the world when the cables flashed from land to land the terrible tidings that James Chalmers, the most picturesque and romantic figure in the religious life of his time, had been killed and eaten by the Fly River cannibals. It is the evening of Easter Sunday. It has for years been the dream of his life to navigate the Fly River and evangelize the villages along its banks. And now he is actually doing it at last. "He is away up the Fly River," wrote Robert Louis Stevenson. "It is a desperate venture, but he is quite a Livingstone card!" Stevenson thought Chalmers all gold. "He is a rowdy, but he is a hero. You can't weary me of that fellow. He is as big as a house and far bigger than any church. He took me fairly by storm for the most attractive, simple, brave and interesting man in the whole Pacific." "I wonder," Stevenson wrote to Mrs. Chalmers, "I wonder if even *you* know what it means to a man like *me* — a man fairly critical, a man of the world — to meet one who represents the essential, and who is so free from the formal, from the grimace."

But I digress. As Stevenson says, Mr. Chalmers is away up the Fly River, a desperate venture! But he is boisterously happy about it, and at sunset on this Easter Sunday evening they anchor off a populous settlement just around the bend of the river. The natives, coming off in their canoes, swarm on to the vessel. With some difficulty Mr. Chalmers persuades them to leave the ship, promising them that he will himself visit them at daybreak. The savages, bent on treachery and slaughter, pull ashore and quickly dispatch runners with messages to all the villages around.

When, early next morning, Mr. Chalmers lands, he is surprised at finding a vast assemblage gathered to receive him. He is accompanied by Mr. Tomkins — his young colleague, not long out from England — and by a party of ten native Christians. They are told that a great feast has been prepared in their honor, and they are led to a large native house to partake of it. But, as he enters, Mr. Chalmers is felled from behind with a stone club, stabbed with a cassowary dagger, and instantly beheaded. Mr. Tomkins and the native Christians are similarly massacred. The villages around are soon the scenes of horrible cannibal orgies.

"I cannot believe it!" exclaimed Dr. Parker from the pulpit of the City Temple, on the day on which the tragic news reached England, "I cannot believe it! I do not want to believe it! Such a mystery of Providence makes it hard for our strained faith to recover itself. Yet Jesus was murdered. Paul was murdered. Many missionaries have been murdered. When I think of *that* side of the case, I cannot but feel that our honored and noble-minded friend has joined a great assembly. James Chalmers was one of the truly great missionaries of the world. He was, in all respects, a noble and kingly character."

And so it was whispered from lip to lip that James Chalmers, the Greatheart of New Guinea, was dead, dead, dead; although John Oxenham denied it.

> Greatheart is dead, they say!
> Greatheart is dead, they say!
>   Nor dead, nor sleeping! He lives on! His name
>   Shall kindle many a heart to equal flame;
>
>   The fire he kindled shall burn on and on
>   Till all the darkness of the lands be gone,
>   And all the kingdoms of the earth be won,
>   And one!
> A soul so fiery sweet can never die
> But lives and loves and works through all eternity.

Yes, *lives* and *loves* and *works!* "There will be much to do in heaven," he wrote to an old comrade in one of the last letters he ever penned. "I guess I shall have good mission work to do; great, brave work for Christ! He will have to find it, for I can be nothing else than a missionary!" And so, perchance, James Chalmers is a missionary still!

IV

Now, underlying this brave story of a noble life and a martyr-death is a great principle; and it is the principle that, if we look, we shall find embedded in the very heart of James Chalmers' text. No law of life is more vital.

Let us return to that evangelistic meeting held on that drenching night at Inverary, and let us catch once more those matchless cadences that won the heart of Chalmers! *"The Spirit and the Bride say, Come; and let him that heareth say, Come; and let him that is a-thirst come; and whosoever will, let him take the water of life freely."*

"Let him that is athirst come!" "I was athirst," says Chalmers, "so I came!"

"Let him that heareth say, Come!" James Chalmers *heard*; he felt that he must *say;* that is the connecting link between the evangelistic meeting at Inverary and the triumph and tragedy of New Guinea.

"Let him that heareth, say!" — that is the principle embedded in the text. The soul's exports must keep pace with the soul's imports. What I have freely received, I must as freely give. The boons that have descended to me from a remote ancestry I must pass on with interest to a remote posterity. The benedictions that my parents breathed on me must be conferred by me upon my children. *"Let him that heareth, say!"* What comes into the City of Mansoul at Ear Gate must go out again at Lip Gate. The auditor of one day must become the orator of the next. It is a very ancient principle. "He that reads," says the prophet, "must run!" "He that sees must spread!"

With those quick eyes of his, James Chalmers saw this at a glance. He recognized that the kingdom of Christ could be established in no other way. He saw that the Gospel could have been offered him on no other terms. What, therefore, he had with such wonder heard, he began, with great delight, to proclaim.

Almost at once he accepted a Sunday school class; the following year he began preaching in those very villages through which, as a boy, his exploratory wanderings had so often taken him; a year later he became a city missionary, that he might pass on the message of the Spirit and the Bride to the teeming poor of Glasgow; and, twelve months later still, he entered college, in order to equip himself for service in the uttermost ends of the earth. His boyish passion for books and boxes had been sanctified at last by his consecration to a great heroic mission.

V

"Let him that is athirst come!" "I was athirst," says Chalmers,

"and I came!"

"Let him that heareth say, Come!" And Chalmers, having heard, said, "Come!" and said it with effect. Dr. Lawes speaks of one hundred and thirty mission stations which he established at New Guinea. And look at this! "On the first Sabbath in every month not less than three thousand men and women gather devotedly round the table of the Lord, reverently commemorating the event which means so much to them and to all the world. Many of them were known to Chalmers as savages in feathers and war-paint. Now, clothed and in their right mind, the wild, savage look all gone, they form part of the Body of our Lord Jesus Christ and are members of His Church. Many of the pastors who preside at the Lord's Table bear on their breasts the tattoo marks that indicate that their spears had been imbrued with human blood. Now sixty-four of them, thanks to Mr. Chalmers' influence, are teachers, preachers, and missionaries."

They, too, having listened, proclaim; having received, give; having heard, say; having been auditors, have now become orators. They have read and therefore they run. Having believed with the heart, they therefore confess with the mouth. This is not only a law of life; it is the law of the life everlasting. It is only by loyalty to this golden rule, on the part of all who hear the Spirit and the Bride say Come, that the kingdoms of this world can become the kingdoms of our God and of His Christ. It is the secret of world-conquest; and, besides it, there is no other.

I have somewhere read that, out in the solitudes of the great dusty desert, when a caravan is in peril of perishing for want of water, they give one camel its head and let him go. The fine instincts of the animal will lead him unerringly to the refreshing spring. As soon as he is but a speck on the horizon, one of the Arabs mounts his camel and sets off in the direction that the liberated animal has taken. When, in his turn, he is scarcely distinguishable, another Arab mounts and follows. When the loose camel discovers water, the first Arab turns and waves to the second; the second to the third, and so on, until all the members of the party are gathered at the satisfying spring. As each man sees the beckoning hand, he turns and beckons to the man behind him. He that sees, signals; he that hears, utters. It is the law of life everlasting; it is the fundamental principle of James Chalmers' text and of James Chalmers' life.

"Let him that is athirst come!" "I was athirst," says Chalmers, "so I came!"

I heard the voice of Jesus say,
  "Behold, I freely give
The living water; thirsty one
  Stoop down, and drink, and live."
I came to Jesus, and I drank
  Of that life-giving stream;
My thirst was quenched, my soul revived,
  And now I live in Him.

"And now I live in Him." The life that James Chalmers lived in his Lord was a life so winsome that he charmed all hearts, a life so contagious that savages became saints beneath his magnetic influence. He had heard, at Inverary, the Spirit and the Bride say, *"Come!"* And he esteemed it a privilege beyond all price to be permitted to make the abodes of barbarism and the habitations of cruelty re-echo the matchless music of that mighty monosyllable.